WHO

IN

THE BRITISH MONARCHY

From

The Saxon Kings

to

Elizabeth II

By

DAVID HILLIAM

POCKET REFERENCE BOOKS

Published by:
Pocket Reference Books Publishing Ltd.
Premier House
Hinton Road
Bournemouth
Dorset BH1 2EF

First published 1996

Typesetting: Gary Tomlinson
PrintRelate (Bournemouth, Dorset)
(01202) 897659

Cover Design: Van Renselar Bonney Design Associates

Printing and Binding: RPM Reprographics
Units 2-3 Spur Road
Quarry Lane, Chichester
West Sussex PO19 2PR
Tel. 01243 787077
Fax. 01243 780012
Modem 01243 536482
E-Mail: rpm@argonet.co.uk

ISBN: 1 899437 56 8

Contents **Pages**

ALL POCKET REFERENCE BOOKS INCLUDE A FREE FULL PAGE ADVERTISEMENT ON THE INSIDE FRONT COVER FOR A WELL-KNOWN CHARITY SELECTED BY THE AUTHOR

INTRODUCTION

The British Monarchy has changed enormously over the centuries. The difference between the savage warrior-kings of Saxon times and the sophisticated constitutional monarchs of today is astonishing.

This account of all the Kings and Queens of Britain is an attempt to show the unfolding story of royalty and how it has developed.

When William the Conqueror was crowned, he could claim quite literally to 'own' the kingdom. He could do what he wanted. And did.

Bit by bit, however, owing to a multitude of events and personalities, this absolute power has been lessened. Magna Carta, the growth of Parliament, the effects of weak kings and rebellious rivals, civil wars, foreign kings who could not speak English, increased voting rights: all these have led to our present 'Constitutional Monarchy', and it is useful to remind ourselves what this implies.

First and foremost, it means that the monarch **reigns** and does not **rule**.

This is an important and subtle distinction. It means that although the monarch possesses no direct political, judicial or executive power, he or she presides over those who do. In practical terms, although the monarch has no absolute power, his or her existence prevents other people from getting it. No ruthless politician could ever become an unrestrained dictator in Great Britain.

This may seem somewhat theoretical, but abuse of power must be checked, and this position of a sovereign is a practical safeguard.

The monarch today as Head of State represents the country, acting as a visible symbol of the nation's history. Being politically neutral, the monarch provides stability in times of crisis, and continuity during periods of change.

In moments of grief, pride, remembrance and celebration, the institution of the monarchy is much more important than any individual king or queen. Changes are bound to occur, but whatever happens in the future, we need to take heed of the lessons of the past.

Clearly this book has been able to deal only briefly with each King or Queen, but we hope that it will act as a guide for those who wish to know more about these fascinating personalities and about others who have been involved in British History.

David Hilliam

TEASERS

WHAT DO YOU KNOW ABOUT THE BRITISH MONARCHS? TRY THESE TEASERS

Which king had twenty-one bastards? *(25)*

Which queen is depicted on every pack of playing cards? *(94)*

Who founded Westminster Abbey? *(21)*

Which king ordered Brighton Pavilion to be built? *(66)*

Which English king and queen were married in Cyprus? *(29)*

Which king invented a clock? *(13)*

Who reigned as joint monarchs? *(60)*

Which English queen was buried in an old arrow-chest? *(95)*

Which king had tea with Hitler? *(107)*

Which king gained his nickname from his red hair? *(24)*

Who married two kings of England and had two sons who were also kings of England? *(81)*

Which king was 9 months old when he came to the throne? *(38)*

Which king was 59 when he came to the throne? *(70)*

Who was the mother of Queen Elizabeth I? *(50)*

Who was the mother of Queen Mary I? *(48)*

Who 'invented' the 'House of Windsor' as a royal name? *(71)*

Which king had fifteen legitimate children? *(65)*

Which queen was put in prison, accused of being a witch? *(91)*

Who ordered the execution of Mary, Queen of Scots? *(51)*

Which teenage monarch founded many grammar schools? *(46)*

What does the 'Tudor Rose' signify? *(42)*

Who founded King's College, Cambridge? *(38)*

Who became known as 'the Grandmother of Europe'? *(69)*

Which king was murdered by his stepmother queen? *(17)*

Which king was crowned, aged 9, with his mother's golden collar? *(86)*

(Answers are to be found on the pages indicated)

Dates of accession are given:
"his" or "her" refers to the preceding monarch.

SAXON KINGS of ENGLAND

Egbert	802
Ethelwulf (his son)	839
Ethelbald (his son)	858
Ethelbert (his brother)	860
Ethelred I (his brother)	865
Alfred the Great (his brother)	871
Edward the Elder (his son)	899
Athelstan (his son)	924
Edmund I (his half-brother)	939
Edred (his brother)	946
Edwy (his nephew)	955
Edgar (his brother)	959
Edward (Saint) (his son)	975
Ethelred II (his half-brother)	978
Edmund (his son)	1016

DANISH KINGS OF ENGLAND

Canute	1016
Harold I (his son)	1035
Hardicanute (his half-brother)	1040

SAXON KINGS OF ENGLAND (Restored)

Edward the Confessor	1042
Harold II	1066

NORMAN KINGS OF ENGLAND

William the Conqueror	1066
William Rufus (his son)	1087
Henry I (his brother)	1100
Stephen (his nephew)	1135
(Matilda, Henry I's daughter)	1141

PLANTAGENET KINGS OF ENGLAND

Henry II (son of Matilda)	1154
Richard I (Lionheart)	1189
John (his brother)	1199
Henry III (his son)	1216
Edward I (his son)	1272
Edward II (his son)	1307
Edward III (his son)	1327
Richard II (his grandson, and son of the Black Prince)	1377
Henry IV (grandson of Ed. III)	1399
Henry V (his son)	1413
Henry VI (his son)	1422-61 & 1470-71
Edward IV (his distant cousin)	1461-1470 & 1471-1483
Edward V (his son)	1483
Richard III (his uncle, and brother of Edward IV)	1483

TUDOR MONARCHS OF ENGLAND

Henry VII	1485
Henry VIII (his son)	1509
Edward VI (his son)	1547
Lady Jane Grey	1553
Mary I (Edward's half-sister)	1553
Elizabeth I (her half-sister)	1558

STUART MONARCHS OF ENGLAND

James I	1603
Charles I (his son)	1625-1649
(Oliver Cromwell, Protector)	
Charles II (Charles I's son)	1660
James II (his brother)	1685
William III and Mary II	1689
(Mary was James II's daughter)	
Anne (Mary's sister)	1702

HANOVERIAN MONARCHS OF ENGLAND

George I (great grandson of James I)	1714
George II (his son)	1727
George III (his grandson)	1760
George IV (his son)	1820
William IV (his brother)	1830

HOUSE OF SAXE-COBURG-GOTHA

Victoria (grand-daughter of George III)	1837
Edward VII (her son)	1901
George V (his son)	1910

HOUSE OF WINDSOR (name adopted in 1917)

Edward VIII (George V's son)	1936
George VI (his brother)	1936
Elizabeth II (his daughter)	1952

THE VERY DISTANT PAST

Just after the Romans left Britain

The story of Britain immediately after the Romans left is rather shadowy and confusing.

When the last Roman ship left these shores about 410 AD there was an awkward power-vacuum. Total chaos prevailed, and various petty chieftains squabbled among themselves for tiny kingdoms.

One of these rulers, Vortigern, was so desperate for help that about the year 450 AD he imported help from the continent to beat off northern tribesmen who were troubling him.

This was the signal. Not only did these helpers come, but they stayed. Boatload after boatload of eager immigrants came: Angles, Saxons, Jutes, Frisians, Franks. The Anglo-Saxon invasion had begun.

The native Britons, or Celts, were pushed further and further into the fringes of the British Isles – into Cornwall, Wales, Scotland. Meanwhile there was a frantic free-for-all as the Saxon boatloads seized whatever bits of land they could.

Naturally, there was opposition from the native Celts, and the almost legendary King Arthur was one of the leaders in trying to beat off the advancing Saxons. However, nothing could stop them arriving and settling.

After a century or so, in about 550 AD, there were probably as many as 1,000 little Saxon 'kingdoms', some only a few square miles in area. There's very little to see nowadays as a reminder of those years, but we do have some clues about the local chieftains of that time in the place-names which still survive.

Look on a map of England and see what a large number of towns and villages have names ending in -ING, or -INGHAM, or -INGTON. The word *ingas* meant 'family' or 'followers', so that when a boatload landed, the chief's name (say, Tota, Wocca, Haefer, or Padda) would be perpetuated in the name of the spot where he carved out his little kingdom, and this would be followed by -ING to show that Tota's family or Wocca's followers had settled there with him. Tooting, Woking, Havering and Paddington are typical examples.

A *ham* meant 'home' or 'homestead', and a *tun* was 'enclosure' and later came to mean 'village' or 'town'. So a village with a name such as Donington would suggest that it was the 'town where Dunna's people live'.

Gradually these tiny settlements grouped into larger units, and eventually, in the sixth century, just seven major Anglo-Saxon kingdoms emerged. And then, in the year 825, these seven kingdoms at last became united under the dominant King Egbert of Wessex.

Egbert, therefore, is regarded as the very first king of a united England. But first, let's look at those seven Saxon kingdoms.

THE SEVEN SAXON KINGDOMS

The seven Saxon Kingdoms each lasted for about three hundred years, until finally King Egbert of Wessex was hailed as 'Bretwalda' or 'sole ruler of Britain" round about the year 825 AD.

For this reason, Egbert is generally recognised as the first English king, and it is possible to trace a line of descent from him right down to our present Queen Elizabeth II.

The seven Saxon Kingdoms were : Kent, East Anglia, Essex, Sussex, Mercia, Northumberland and Wessex.

The 'sex' part of these names is simply a shortened form of 'Saxon', so that 'Essex' means the 'East Saxons, 'Sussex' means 'South Saxons' and of course 'Wessex' means 'West Saxons'.

KENT is reckoned to have been the first Saxon kingdom, founded shortly after Vortigern's invitation to the continental communities to come to his aid. The first Kentish Kings were the brothers Hengist and Horsa. Unfortunately Horsa was killed in battle, but Hengist ruled Kent from about 455 to 488 AD. Thereafter, a line of 17 Kentish kings ruled this part of England, until it acknowledged King Egbert in 825.

EAST ANGLIA had a series of sixteen kings, called 'Wuffings', after their first king, Wuffa. The last king of East Anglia was St Edmund, after whom the city of Bury St Edmunds is named.

ESSEX had a line of fifteen kings before acknowledging Egbert in 825.

SUSSEX had a line of nine kings, but the records are incomplete.

MERCIA's line of kings is also incomplete, but fifteen kings are recorded before Egbert was acknowledged. One of the Mercian kings was the famous and influential King Offa, who constructed a 120-mile long earthwork to protect his kingdom from the Welsh.

NORTHUMBRIA had a line of twenty-five kings until its King Eanred did homage to Egbert in 827.

And finally, **WESSEX** had its own line of nineteen kings, leading to Egbert.

The first king of Wessex was CERDIC, who reigned from 519 to 534 AD. After him came eighteen kings. Egbert, therefore, can be seen as the 19th king of Wessex as well as the first king of England.

Relatively little is known about some of these kings of Wessex, but some of them were great men, who ruled valiantly in difficult times. For your interest, and for the sake of completeness, here is the line of Wessex Kings stretching from Cerdic to Egbert. ('His' refers to the immediate predecessor).

Kings of the West Saxons

(i.e. Wessex)

Dates given are the years in which these kings reigned

Cerdic	519-534	first King of Wessex
Cynric	534-560	his son
Ceawlin	560-591	his son
Ceol	591-597	
Ceolwulf	597-611	his brother
Cynegils	611-643	
Cenwalh	643-672	his son
Seaxburgh	672-674	his wife
Cenfus	674	grandson of Ceolwulf
Aescwine	674-676	his son
Centwine	676-685	brother of Cenwalh
Cadwalla	685-688	desc. from Ceawlin
Ine	688-726	
Ethelheard	726-740	
Cuthred	740-756	
Sigeberht	756-757	
Cynewulf	757-786	
Beohrtric	786-802	
Egbert	802-839	

Including these early Wessex rulers, then, the line of succession of English Monarchs stretches from
CERDIC TO THE HOUSE OF WINDS0R

This is a time-span of almost fifteen centuries

THE REIGNING KINGS AND QUEENS OF ENGLAND

EGBERT

Reigned 802-839 – Born c770; died 839

Egbert was King of the West Saxons who gradually forced his dominance over the other Saxon Kingdoms. He defeated the Mercians at the Battle of Ellandune (near Swindon) in 825 and was acknowledged as 'Bretwalda' or 'King of Britain' by the other Saxon kingdoms (Kent, Sussex, Essex, Northumbria, East Anglia) at that important date.

Various kings of some of these Saxon kingdoms continued to exist, so the dominance was not entirely clearcut; nevertheless, Egbert is considered to be the first overall King of England.

His bones lie in a chest near the altar in Winchester Cathedral.

ETHELWULF

Reigned 839-858 – Born c800; died 858

Son of Egbert. Crowned at Kingston-upon-Thames; had been 'sub-king' of Kent; was Bishop of Winchester for a while; fought against the Danes and won a victory at Oakley in Surrey and won another battle at sea; took his son, the future Alfred the Great, on a pilgrimage to Rome; married Charlemagne's 13-year-old granddaughter Judith (his second marriage); and yielded the throne to his son Ethelbald.

ETHELBALD

Reigned 856-860 – Born c834; died 860

Son of Ethelwulf. Crowned at Kingston-upon-Thames; married his father's widow Judith (she was still only 15), and as this was illegal Judith's father, King Charles the Bald of France, demanded her back and put her in a nunnery. (Judith later eloped, married again, and became ancestress of Matilda of Flanders, wife of William the Conqueror.).

Ethelbald was buried at Sherborne Abbey in Dorset.

ETHELBERT

Reigned 860-865 – Born c836; died 865

Ethelbald's younger brother. Crowned at Kingston-upon-Thames; during his reign the Danes were creating havoc in the south east and destroyed Winchester in 860. Like his predecessor brother, he was buried at Sherborne Abbey.

ETHELRED I

Reigned 865-871 – Born c840; died 871

Ethelbert's younger brother. Crowned at Kingston-upon-Thames; known as a saint; fought eight battles against the Danes; died of wounds after the Battle of Merton in Oxfordshire; buried in Wimborne Minster in Dorset. Succeeded by his younger brother, one of the most outstanding kings in history, Alfred the Great.

QUEEN BOUDICCA

(lst century AD)

(Until recently her name was spelt as Boadicea, but now Boudicca is considered correct)

There is a dramatic statue opposite the Houses of Parliament, at the end of Westminster Bridge, showing Boudicca in her chariot. She would have been amazed to know that she would be so honoured in a city which she totally destroyed.

She was the queen of a British (Celtic) tribe known as the Iceni, who lived in East Anglia in the early years of the Roman occupation. Her husband, Prasutagus, had come to friendly terms with the Emperor Nero, but when he died, in AD 60, the Roman soldiers seized all his territory and flogged and raped Boudicca and her daughters.

Boudicca, seething with revenge, led an army of the Iceni to destroy the Roman camps at Colchester, St Albans and London. She burned, sacked, pillaged, and managed to kill 70,000 Roman soldiers. Their camp in London was in ruins.

Naturally, the Romans counter-attacked. They had to re-assemble their legions, and defeated Boudicca in a battle somewhere in the Midlands. It is recorded that 80,000 Iceni were killed as against only 400 Roman soldiers.

Boudicca committed suicide by poisoning herself.

ALFRED THE GREAT

Reigned 871-899

Born c849 in Wantage, Berkshire
Died 26.10.99 in Winchester
Son of Ethelwulf
Married to Elswitha – Two sons and three daughters

The only appropriate title for Alfred is "the Great'". He was an outstanding Saxon King, and would have made a brilliant monarch in any age.

As a boy he had been twice to Rome and had been an honoured guest of Pope Leo IV, who confirmed him, so he had a broader vision of European culture than most of his predecessors.

He was the youngest of the family; three of his brothers had been Saxon kings before him; then, after helping his brother King Ethelred to fight eight battles against the Danes, he had the sadness of seeing him die of wounds after the Battle of Merton. He was elected king as Ethelred's sons were still too young to command authority.

The first years of his reign were desperate. The Danes were moving further and further into the west of England. In January 878 they made a surprise attack and gained even more territory, so that Alfred had to go into hiding in marshy land near Athelney, in Somerset. This is where the story of 'Alfred and the cakes' is supposed to have taken place (disguised as an ordinary traveller, he stayed for a while in a swineherd's cottage, and after letting some cakes burn, which he had been asked to look after, earned a sharp rebuke from the swineherd's wife, who of course did not know who he was).

Ironically, the cake episode, which is probably invention, is remembered more than many of his real achievements.

Patiently and with great courage and tenacity, Alfred gathered his army together again and fought one of the most important battles in English history, the Battle of Edington, near Westbury in Wiltshire, in May 878. It was ferocious fighting with swords and axes, lasting for many hours. However, the Danes were decisively defeated, and the threat to Wessex was halted.

But the most interesting thing about this victory was the way in which Alfred dealt with the defeated Danish leader Guthrum and the remains of his army. Alfred pursued them back to their camp at Wedmore, near Bath, and surrounded them. He had them completely in his power and could have starved or slaughtered every one of them. They begged for mercy and said he could take as many hostages as he liked if only Alfred would let them go.

Quite astonishingly, Alfred insisted that Guthrum became baptised as a Christian and stood godfather to him; then he entertained the whole Danish army for twelve days and gave them gifts. After this he let them go and had peace for fourteen years.

In 886 Alfred captured London and in the subsequent peace treaty allowed the Danes to stay in East Anglia, but Wessex and the south were left to Alfred.

In the following years Alfred showed himself to be an imaginative and innovative peacetime ruler; in fact it has been said that if he had never fought a battle he would still have been one of Britain's greatest kings.

He reorganised the defences of Wessex and set up a rota-system for military service, so that he could always have a standing army and yet men could also get on with their farming or other jobs in peace. He restored fortresses throughout Wessex and caused new ones to be built, thus founding dozens of new towns. These were 'boroughs' (the Saxon word *burh* meant 'fortress'). The largest of these in Wessex was his capital, Winchester.

Realising that the Danes would still try further invasions, he built large speedy ships, and successfully fought several sea battles. He is generally regarded as being the 'father of the English navy'.

In addition to all this, Alfred revised the laws of the land; introduced many new ones; invited foreign scholars to his court; encouraged learning and the arts; set in motion the writing of the great *Anglo-Saxon Chronicle*; learnt Latin himself and translated books by Boethius, Bede, Gregory the Great, Orosius and St Augustine; invented a clock made with candles; and started the *'Book of Winchester'*, which was a survey of the counties, parishes and hundreds into which he divided his kingdom.

He was only 50 when he died in 901. A thousand years later his great reign was celebrated by the erection of a magnificent statue in Winchester, his capital city. No English king has been given any title other than Alfred the Great.

EDWARD THE ELDER

Reigned 899-924

Born 870

Died, 924 in Farndon-on-Dee in Cheshire

Alfred the Great's son. Crowned at Kingston-upon-Thames; fought successfully against the Danes, capturing the Danish Five Boroughs of Leicester, Stamford, Nottingham, Derby and Lincoln; fortified other towns; fathered two sons by a mistress Egwina, eight children by his wife Elfreda, and two more sons by his wife Edgifu; annexed Mercia after the death of his sister Ethelfleda, who had been its ruler; died and was buried in Winchester.

ATHELSTAN

Reigned 924-939

Born c895

Died, 27.10.939

Son of Edward the Elder and Egwina. Unmarried

Crowned at Kingston-upon-Thames. Althelstan was the first undisputed king of all England, and the Welsh and Scottish kings also paid him homage. He arranged politically advantageous marriages for his sisters: one of them to the Holy Roman Emperor Otto the Great; another to Hugh Capet of France; and another to King Charles of the West Franks.

He was a great king, giving hospitality to other kings, passing humane laws, introducing a national coinage, and administering the unified country with skill.

Apart from being a great soldier and administrator, Athelstan was also a great connoisseur of art, precious Gospel Books and holy relics. His own monastery, Malmesbury Abbey, was a treasure-house of remarkable and beautiful objects, given to him by his many royal foreign friends and relations. Most of these objects were priceless works of art; but some were bogus relics, for example there was a 'piece of the holy and adorable Cross enclosed in a crystal . . . a portion also of the crown of thorns.'

He was buried at Malmesbury, in north Wiltshire and was succeeded by his half-brother.

EDMUND I
(EDMUND THE ELDER)

Reigned 939-946

Born c921

Died 26.5.946 in Pucklechurch, Gloucestershire

Son of Edward the Elder and Edgifu

Married (i) (Saint) Elgifu by whom he had two sons, Edwy and Edgar

Married (ii) Ethelfled of Damerham

Crowned at Kingston-upon-Thames. He was only aged 25 when he was stabbed to death in a brawl. Nevertheless his reign, though brief, was full of incident and he had fought successfully against the Vikings in the Midlands and Northumbria. He was buried at Glastonbury in Somerset, and was succeeded by his brother.

EDRED

Reigned 946-955

Born 923

Died 23.11.955 in Frome, Somerset

Son of Edward the Elder and Edgifu

Crowned at Kingston-upon-Thames. His nine-year reign saw much fighting, especially in the north, where he fought the Dane, Eric Bloodaxe. He established dominance in Northumbria; was advised by St Dunstan, Abbot of Glastonbury, to help establish monastic centres of learning. He is buried in Winchester.

WINCHESTER – BURIAL-PLACE OF KINGS

Six unique mortuary chests are to be seen on top of stone screens near the altar, containing the oldest kingly bones in England. The inscriptions tell us who lie in each chest: 1. Edred (Son of Edward the Elder died 955); 2. Edmund (Son of Alfred the Great); 3. "In this chest and in the one opposite are the remains of Cnut and Rufus, kings; of Emma, queen; and of Wina and Alwyn, bishops." 4. King Kynegils of Wessex, died 641 and King Ethelwulf, died 857; 5. King Kenewalch, died 714, and King Egbert, died 837; 6. "In this chest, in 1661 were promiscuously laid the bones of princes and prelates which had been scattered by sacrilegious barbarism in 1642."

EDWY THE FAIR

Reigned 955- 959

Born c940
Died 1.10.959

Son of Edmund the Elder and Edgifu

Married Elfgivu, his step-mother's daughter

Crowned at Kingston-upon-Thames. He was only 15 when he came to the throne, and nineteen when he was probably murdered. He is notorious for having left his coronation banquet in order to make love to his mistress, and had to be brought back and listen to rebukes from Archbishop Odo.

He married the mistress, but then had to banish her because he was related to her, which made the marriage illegal.

He exiled the famous church leader, Dunstan; lost control of Mercia and Northumbria; was finally forced to give up his throne to his younger brother Edgar.

He died at Gloucester.

EDGAR THE PEACEFUL

Reigned 959-975

Born c944

Died 8.7.975

Son of Edmund the Elder and Edgifu

Married (i) Ethelfled, by whom he had a son, Saint Edward, King and Martyr

(ii) Elfrida, by whom he had a son, Edmund Aethling and Ethelred II

Crowned in Bath. Famous for being rowed in state by eight British (Scottish and Welsh) Kings on the River Dee; brought back Dunstan to become his Archbishop of Canterbury and chief adviser; founded many abbeys; ruled over a peaceful and united country.

Buried at Glastonbury Abbey, Somerset, and was succeeded by his son Edward the Martyr.

EDWARD II
KING AND SAINT (EDWARD THE MARTYR)

Reigned 975-978

Born c963
Died 18.3.978 at Corfe Castle, Dorset
Son of Edgar and Ethelfled

Crowned at Kingston-upon-Thames. He was about thirteen when his father Edgar died and was king for less than three years.

He was murdered on the orders of his step-mother Elfrida when he went to visit her at Corfe Castle. She wanted to place her own son Ethelred on the throne.

The murder was a bloody affair, and shortly afterwards miracles were said to happen at his tomb. Thus he became known as a saint and martyr.

He was buried first at Wareham and then at Shaftesbury. His bones are now kept as holy relics in a Russian Orthodox Church in Brookwood, Surrey.

ETHELRED THE UNREADY

Reigned 978-1016

Born c968
Died 23.4.1016 in London
Son of Edgar I and Elfrida
Married (i) Elfred of Northumbria, by whom he had Edmund II and about five other children
(ii) Emma of Normandy, by whom he had Edward the Confessor and two other children

Crowned at Kingston-upon-Thames. The title or nickname 'The Unready' means that he was ***unraed***, which is Saxon for 'ill-advised' or 'lacking advice'. Certainly he was ill-advised to try to buy off the Danes and Vikings. He spent enormous sums in protection money; then he tried massacring the Danish settlers; finally he had to flee the country when the Danish King Sweyn invaded England.

Sweyn ruled briefly as uncrowned king but soon died. Ethelred was brought back, but then he too died, was buried in the Saxon St Paul's in London and the throne passed to his son Edmund Ironside.

EDMUND II
(EDMUND IRONSIDE)

Reigned April to November 1016

Born c992

Died 30.11.1016 in London

Son of Ethelred the Unready and Elfled

Married Eadgyth and had two sons

Crowned at Old St Paul's Cathedral, London. Struggling against the Danes, Edmund fought four battles, won three, but then was let down by the Mercians and had to partition the country, sharing it with the Danish King Canute, son of Sweyn Forkbeard.

Edmund died soon after, probably murdered, and so the throne was left entirely to the Danes, led by King Canute.

Edmund was buried in Glastonbury Abbey in Somerset.

SWEYN FORKBEARD

Reigned briefly in 1013-1014

Sweyn Forkbeard often attacked England from about 994 onwards.

In 1013 he invaded in earnest, driving Ethelred II from the throne. He reigned for a few weeks only, being killed after falling from his horse.

His death paved the way for his son, Canute, otherwise spelt as Cnut.

LONDON BRIDGE IS FALLING DOWN . . .

Olaf was a Norwegian warrior who in 1014 helped the Saxon King Ethelred recapture London from the Danes, who had taken the city in 1013.

Olaf recaptured London in a spectacular way, by sailing up the Thames as far as London Bridge, tying ropes to the piles, and then getting his men to row off downstream. The bridge must have been in a very weak state, because this manoeuvre resulted in toppling London Bridge down and all the Danish defenders fell into the Thames.

Nowadays we still remember this dramatic battle in the old nursery rhyme, "London Bridge is falling down." Olaf became King of Norway and a saint. Five London churches were dedicated to him.

CANUTE

Reigned 1016-1035

Born c992

Died 12.11.1035 in Shaftesbury, Dorset

Son of Sweyn Forkbeard and Gunhild of Poland

Married (i) Elgifu of Northampton by whom he had two sons, including Harold I (Harold Harefoot)

(ii) Emma of Normandy, widow of Ethelred the Unready, by whom he had Hardicanute and a daughter, Gunhild

Canute was a great king. Although arguably he was a 'foreign invader' he brought peace and stability to the country and ruled wisely and well. Nowadays, his name is often spent as Cnut.

He had fought Edmund Ironside and had forced him to partition the country, but then when Edmund died he was sole ruler for almost twenty years.

This rule was supported by the Saxon ***Witan*** or parliament, and he was crowned in St Paul's in London.

He was also King of Norway and Denmark, but spent most of his time in England, living in Winchester, the old capital.

He was a strong believer in Christianity and made a pilgrimage to Rome. The story of 'Canute and the waves', in which he is reputed to have shown his flattering courtiers that even he could not control the tides, is probably the only thing that many people remember about him.

Another version of the story, less well known, tells of how Canute subdued Saxon rebels in Southampton who were reputed to use sorcery to control the tides. He captured them, bound them to stakes on the sea-shore, and watched as the tide rolled in and drowned them. Thus he proved that the Saxon superstitions were worthless, and that his own Christian beliefs were supreme.

In Winchester it is told how, after this episode with the waves, he rode his horse up the aisle of the cathedral and placed his golden crown on the high altar, in token that only God was powerful enough to rule the elements. It is said that Canute's golden crown disappeared only at the time of the Reformation.

A master-stroke was to marry Emma, the widow of Ethelred the Unready. He was strong, popular, and maintained good trade relations with the continent. The pair lived happily together for seventeen years.

Canute's bones lie still in the cathedral at Winchester.

HAROLD I
(HAROLD HAREFOOT)

Reigned 1035-1040

Born 1016

Died 17.3.1040 in Oxford

Son of Canute and Elfgifu

Unmarried

Harold was crowned at Oxford. His was a short and brutal reign. He exiled his step-mother Emma to Bruges, and is generally reputed to said to have blinded and murdered Ethelred's son Alfred, who was a possible rival to the throne.

It was no great loss to the country when he died aged about 24. His claim to the throne was debatable: he was succeeded by his half brother, Hardicanute.

HARDICANUTE

Reigned 1040-1042

Born 1018

Died 8.6.1042 in Lambeth, London

Son of Canute and Emma of Normandy

Crowned at Canterbury. Arguably, Hardicanute should have succeeded his father instead of Harold I, so he showed what he thought of Harold by ordering his dead body to be dug up, his head to be cut off and thrown into the Thames. Luckily, some fishermen managed to drag it out of the river, and it was buried in the cemetery of St. Clement Danes in London.

He murdered Earl Edwulf of Northumbria; burned the city of Worcester; plundered and taxed his subjects to excess. Was thoroughly hated.

He died of a drinking-fit while at a wedding feast and was buried at Winchester. Rumour had it that he was poisoned.

Emma's son, Edward the Confessor, who had been brought up in Normandy, was now invited to become the next king, thus restoring the Saxon line.

EDWARD THE CONFESSOR
(Saint)

Reigned 1042-1066

Born c1003 Islip, near Oxford
Died 5.1.1066 in Westminster

Son of Ethelred the Unready and Emma of Normandy

Married Edith, daughter of Earl Godwin

No children

Edward was regarded as the Patron Saint of England for many centuries, and his lasting importance lies in the fact that he founded Westminster Abbey.

He was the child of mixed cultures: his father, Ethelred, was Saxon, but his mother, Emma, was Norman.

In fact, Edward the Confessor ('confessor' means priest), paved the way for Norman conquest by introducing many Norman ways into England.

Duke William of Normandy, soon to become William the Conqueror, was his great-nephew and friend, and it seems that Edward had promised to make William his heir.

Throughout his life Edward had a great reputation for holiness and for powers of healing people by laying his hands on them. Thus he began the royal custom of 'touching' sufferers and allegedly curing them of their diseases.

Early on in life he had taken a vow of chastity, so was believed to have refused to consummate his marriage. Not surprisingly, he had no heir.

Unworldly as he was, he did not concern himself greatly with the day-to-day running of affairs, and was content to let his father-in-law, Earl Godwin, exercise power in governing the country.

He lived to see the completion of Westminster Abbey, but was far too ill to attend its opening ceremony on December 28 1065.

He died only a few days later, on January 5 1066, and was the first person to be buried there. His bones lie there still, just behind the altar.

HAROLD II

Reigned for 9 months in 1066

Born c1020

Died 14.10.1066 at Senlac, near Hastings

Son of Godwin, Earl of Wessex, and Gytha

His mistress was Edith of the Swan Neck – His wife was Aldgyth

Four sons and two daughters by Edith

A son by Aldgyth

No real claim to the throne, but was brother-in-law of Edward the Confessor

Immediately after the funeral of Edward the Confessor Harold had himself elected King. Literally within hours he was crowned in the same building, Westminster Abbey, that had just witnessed Edward's burial.

Harold had been named by Edward the Confessor as his heir, but there were at least two other claimants to the throne. In fact, Harold had once been forced into making a promise to support Duke William of Normandy. He had been stranded in Normandy at the time and was in William's power. He was tricked into making an oath over holy relics and had sworn future allegiance to William.

The other main claimant to the throne was Hardrada, King of Norway.

Harold's short reign was to be that of the last Saxon King. In September Hardrada and Harold's own brother Tostig joined in an invasion in the north. Harold force-marched his army 200 miles to meet them, and fought a bloody battle at Stamford Bridge, near York, in which he defeated and killed both Hardrada and Tostig.

It was just as he was celebrating his victory at Stamford Bridge that Harold learned that his other enemy, William of Normandy, had landed on the south coast.

Quickly he forced his tired soldiers to march back to fight another battle. It was 250 miles to Hastings, and they got there in nine days, exhausted.

Harold's army was defeated at the Battle of Hastings, 14 October 1066. Harold himself was killed, together with his three other brothers, and Duke William claimed the throne as King William I – usually referred to as William the Conqueror.

WILLIAM I
(WILLIAM THE CONQUEROR)

Reigned 1066-1087

Born 1027 or 1028 in Falaise, France

Died 9.9.1087 near Rouen, France

Married Matilda of Flanders

Four sons, five daughters

William the Conqueror was the illegitimate son of Robert the Devil, Duke of Normandy, and Arlette, teenage daughter of a local tanner in Falaise.

William was the great-nephew of Edward the Confessor, and it is believed that Edward had promised William to make him his heir. On his death-bed Edward seems to have forgotten this by naming Harold as his successor. However, William never forgot King Edward the Confessor's promise to him; neither did he forget that Harold himself had sworn allegiance to him when he had been shipwrecked in Normandy and had been in William's power.

William was clear that he was claiming England by right when he invaded in 1066. The defeat of Harold's army at Hastings was complete, and William had himself crowned in Westminster Abbey on Christmas Day of that year.

The story of the conquest after 1066 is one of ruthless force. Local revolts were fiercely suppressed, especially the opposition in East Anglia led by Hereward the Wake. William pushed into Wales, into Scotland, and in about six or seven years Norman rule was virtually complete.

In order to get a clear idea of what he owned he ordered a complete inventory of all lands and buildings throughout the kingdom, later to be known as the Domesday Book. It is a fascinating account of England at that time.

Then, in 1086 he summoned all landholders to the bleak hill-top fortress of Old Sarum, the old city of Salisbury, to swear allegiance to him in a ceremony we now call the Oath of Salisbury.

To make sure of the support of the church, William replaced the Saxon Archbishop of Canterbury, Stigand, with his own chaplain Lanfranc who quickly transformed the Church along Norman lines.

The Normans were the greatest builders of their times. William's most famous personal contribution was the Tower of London, and at the same time he also began to build Windsor Castle, choosing the site himself.

Scores of castles, churches and cathedrals were built on William's orders, and much of the Saxon heritage was unceremoniously destroyed.

William died after falling from his horse in Mantes, France, aged 60, leaving his English throne to his second son, William Rufus.

WILLIAM II
(WILLIAM RUFUS)

Reigned 1087-1100

Born c1056 in France

Died 2.8.1100, killed in the New Forest, Hampshire

William II got his nickname, Rufus, because of his flaming ginger hair and his ruddy complexion.

Although he was William the Conqueror's second son, he inherited the throne of England by will of his father. His elder brother Robert received the Dukedom of Normandy, and his younger brother Henry (later to become Henry I) was simply given money.

William Rufus's reign was filled with rebellions, skirmishes, deceit, broken promises and violence. No one has spoken well of Rufus either during his lifetime or since.

He sneered at Christianity and when church posts fell vacant he refused to fill them, seizing the money for himself.

One positive and valuable legacy from Rufus, however, is Westminster Hall, for he was directly and personally responsible for this historic building.

William was a known homosexual, and was roundly condemned for his lifestyle by the church. The Archbishop of Canterbury, Anselm, had to flee the country and live in exile for his out-spokenness.

Rufus was killed in mysterious circumstances in the New Forest on 2 August 1100. His body was taken on a farm-cart to nearby Winchester Cathedral, where he was buried.

THE DEATH OF RUFUS

The king was killed with an arrow, but who shot it and whether it was deliberately aimed is still open to question. The suspect, Sir Walter Tirel, immediately fled the country.

A charcoal-burner named Purkiss took the body on a cart to Winchester, 'blood dripping from it all the way', and it was buried in the newly-built Norman cathedral. Shortly afterwards, the cathedral tower fell down, and the superstitious monks were convinced that it was the evil influence of the wicked king which was to blame.

HENRY I

Reigned 1100-1135

Born 1068 in Selby, Yorkshire

Died 1.12.1135, near Rouen, France

Married (i) Matilda of Scotland

(ii) Adela of Louvain

Two sons and one daughter by Matilda

Henry was the youngest and cleverest of the Conqueror's sons. He ruled England with firmness and skill for 35 years, but strictly speaking he had no right to be king at all.

When William Rufus was killed the throne should have gone to his elder brother, Robert Curthose, and Henry must have been acutely aware of this. However, he was a supreme opportunist. He too was in the New Forest on the day of Rufus's death, and as soon as he heard about the accident he rushed to London and had himself crowned within three days.

Robert Curthose was away on a crusade at the time, but when he returned he was naturally furious and landed at Portsmouth with an army to defeat Henry. The two brothers met at Alton, in Hampshire, and it says much for Henry's negotiating skills that their armies did not clash.

The truce did not last. Eventually Henry and Robert met in battle and Henry defeated Robert at Tinchebray, about 40 miles west of Avranches in Normandy. Henry captured Robert and established himself as Duke of Normandy, seizing his brother's inheritance.

After this, Henry's long reign in England was a model of firm rule. He enjoyed life to the full, with a wife, three healthy legitimate children, six mistresses and about twenty-one bastards. He still holds the paternity record among English kings, and he was a good parent to them all.

His final years were marred by disaster. His two sons William and Richard were both drowned in the English Channel in a new boat called *'The White Ship*'. In a famous phrase, it is said that Henry 'never smiled again'.

Henry brought peace and order to the kingdom, and strengthened the Norman hold over the land.

Having no legitimate male heir after his sons were drowned, he nominated his daughter Matilda to be his successor.

Henry died of food poisoning and was buried in Reading Abbey, which he himself had founded.

STEPHEN

Reigned 1135-1154

Born c1097 at Blois, France
Died 25.10.1154 at Dover

Son of Adela, daughter of William the Conqueror
and Stephen, Count of Blois and Chartres
One son, two daughters

By general agreement, one of the worst kings we ever had. His reign was a complete disaster, although as a person he seems to have been kindly and easy-going.

As soon as his uncle Henry I was dead he claimed the throne for himself, although he had sworn allegiance to Henry's daughter Matilda.

The whole of Stephen's reign is a confused tangle of civil conflict, with sieges, battles, imprisonments and supporters switching sides. Stephen himself was captured during a skirmish outside Lincoln, and he was imprisoned first in Gloucester and then in Bristol, while Matilda reigned as 'Domina' or 'Lady of the English'.

He was released in exchange for Matilda's half-brother. And then Matilda herself was besieged, captured, and then escaped.

Eventually a compromise was worked out. Stephen was to keep the throne for his life-time, but Matilda's son Henry would succeed him when he died.

Stephen died 25 October 1154 and was buried in Faversham Abbey, in Kent.

HENRY OF BLOIS – A WARLIKE BISHOP OF WINCHESTER

The civil war between Stephen and Matilda had disastrous consequences for the city of Winchester. The Bishop, Henry of Blois, was Stephen's brother, so naturally he was eager to help defeat Matilda.

When Matilda came to the city in 1141 she settled her forces in the royal castle on the high ground above the city. Meanwhile the Bishop gathered his supporters in his own Wolvesey Castle down in the meadows. Matilda laid siege to the Bishop and he retaliated by bombarding Matilda's headquarters with missiles of burning coal.

Unfortunately, the city and its townsfolk lay between the opposing armies and most of the poor citizens of Winchester had their homes completely destroyed.

MATILDA

Reigned February-November 1141

Born February 1102 in London
Died 10.9.1167 near Rouen, France

Married (i) Holy Roman Emperor, Henry V
(ii) Geoffrey IV, Count of Anjou
Three sons by Geoffrey

After the *White Ship* disaster in which Henry I's sons had been drowned, Matilda had been promised the throne. On Henry's death, however, she was swiftly pushed to one side by her cousin Stephen, who seized the throne instead.

For virtually all of Stephen's reign she struggled to assert her rights and for eight months or so in the year 1141 she was to all intents and purposes the Queen of England, being given the title 'Domina' or 'Lady of the English'. However, she was never crowned, and was so domineering and arrogant that she lost much of the goodwill she might have had. Eventually, after a lengthy, hectic and unsuccessful campaign she left England for good.

Her first husband had been the Holy Roman Emperor Henry V, and she had lived in Germany at that time with the title 'Empress'. She is therefore sometimes referred to as 'Empress Matilda'.

Her life was extraordinarily eventful. During the civil war she escaped from Devizes pretending to be a corpse, clothed in a shroud and roped to a bier. On another occasion she escaped from Oxford Castle, being let down from its tower by a rope. It was a snowy winter's night, so she camouflaged herself by wearing white, and managed to cross the ice-covered river and walk six miles through the snow to Wallingford.

Her Emperor husband had died in 1135 and she married again, this time to Geoffrey IV ('The Handsome'), count of Anjou, by whom she had three sons, the most important of whom was to become Henry II of England.

She is therefore mother of the Plantagenet dynasty, the longest in British history.

She is buried in Fontevrault Abbey in France, having lived to see the first thirteen years of the reign of her Plantagenet son, King Henry II.

HENRY II

Reigned 1154-1189

Born 5.3.1133 in Le Mans, France
Died 6.7.1189 in Chinon Castle, France
Son of the Empress Matilda and Count Geoffrey V of Anjou

Married Eleanor of Aquitaine 18.5.1152
Five sons, three daughters

With his strength and organisational skills Henry II was just what England needed after the disastrous reign of Stephen.

He had already inherited the rich lands of Anjou from his father and acquired the French province of Aquitaine from his wife, so that when he came to the English throne, aged 21, he possessed the largest empire in Europe.

Henry was constantly and frenetically on the move to keep a watchful eye over his vast territories. He spent only 13 years of his 34-year reign in England, but insisted that horses were always kept ready for his use in abbeys all over the country. No one knew when he would make his sudden appearances. He seemed to be everywhere at once.

With urgent firmness he forced law and order upon the kingdom. He strengthened the legal system, imposed taxes, and curbed the unruly barons by pulling down their castles.

Henry was an outstanding king, but in a monumental row with the church he met his match in Thomas Becket, Archbishop of Canterbury.

Henry declared that the church was subject to the law of the land, but Becket told him that the church was above it. It was a collision course, and the outcome was dramatic. "Isn't there anyone who'll get rid of this wretched priest?" shouted Henry, in one of his frequent outbursts of temper. And instantly four of his knights, dutifully taking the hint, sped to Canterbury and killed Becket in his own cathedral.

Becket had triumphed, and instantly became venerated as a martyr, was made a saint, and thousands of pilgrims annually came to visit his shrine in Canterbury.

Henry was a great builder of castles: the lower half of the famous Round Tower in Windsor is his. He enlarged the fortifications of Gloucester and Guildford and refounded Waltham Abbey as a penance for Becket's murder.

He was a quick-tempered, energetic king who did much to lay the foundations of law in England, but his sons were constantly leading revolts against him. He died a disillusioned man, embittered by his sons' disloyalty. He is buried in Fontevrault Abbey, France.

RICHARD I

Reigned 1189-1199

Born 8.9.1157 in Oxford
Died 6.4.1199 in Châlus, France
Third son of Henry II and Eleanor of Aquitaine

Married Berengaria of Navarre
No children

Most people remember Richard as 'Coeur de Lion' – the Lion-Hearted; the great crusader, superb in battle against Saladin; cruelly captured and imprisoned on his way home until his faithful minstrel Blondel sang beneath his window and discovered him; hero of Robin Hood.

This set of images is perpetuated by the romantic and idealised statue of Richard I on horseback which stands just outside the Houses of Parliament.

Sadly, however, it has to be admitted that Richard was one of our worst kings. He had no interest in being king; was in England for only a few months of his ten-year reign; and openly admitted he would have sold the whole of London if he could have found a rich enough buyer. And if he could have sold it, he would have spent the proceeds on one of his interminable wars. The Crusades were his main interest in life.

One must agree that he was a daring and energetic soldier, but he did not manage to capture Jerusalem. All he could do was to negotiate a truce with Saladin, to make it possible for Christians to gain access to Jerusalem.

He was captured by the Duke of Austria and held ransom. It took a quarter of every man's annual income in England to raise the necessary money. Pigs were killed, sheep shorn, church plate sold. It was an expensive business.

It was his mother, Eleanor of Aquitaine, who found Richard a wife, Berengaria of Navarre. She brought her to meet Richard in Sicily, on his way to a crusade. However, Richard was homosexual, and although they were married in Cyprus, he had little time for Berengaria. They drifted apart and Berengaria never even set foot in England.

Richard was killed in a petty skirmish in France, and was succeeded by his younger brother, John.

KING JOHN

Reigned 1199-1216

Born 24.12.1167 in Oxford
Died 18.10.1216 in Newark
Youngest son of Henry II and Eleanor of Aquitaine

Married (i) Isabella of Gloucester
(ii) Isabella of Angoulême
Two sons and three daughters by Isabella of Angoulême

John was the youngest child of Henry II and Eleanor of Aquitaine, and so hardly expected to be king. Indeed his very nickname, 'Lackland', suggested that he simply had no resources. His first marriage was a shamelessly loveless affair to a rich heiress.

John has the reputation of being one of the worst kings. He was unpopular in his lifetime, and made repeated attempts to usurp the throne while his elder brother, Richard I was out of the country.

He quarrelled violently with the church, refusing to accept Stephen Langton as Archbishop of Canterbury. The Pope excommunicated John and closed all England's churches.

With more energy than prudence he spent much time and money in trying to impose his will on the Scots, the Irish and the Welsh. His quarrels with the barons led to a major confrontation with them, and finally John was forced to surrender much of his authority as he was forced to sign the 'Magna Carta' at Runnymede, Surrey, in 1215. This was the beginning of the diminution of royal authority. The document gave the church its independence, prevented arbitrary taxes, and made it impossible to be punished, except without trial. The law was to be upheld, even by kings.

Travelling with all his treasure, not trusting to leave it anywhere out of sight, John's luck finally ran out, and he lost wagon-load after wagon-load of valuables in the Norfolk marshes.

Almost immediately afterwards he died, probably poisoned.

He is buried in Worcester cathedral.

MAGNA CARTA

There are four surviving original texts of Magna Carta, the crucial document which John signed at Runnymede.

Two of these texts are in the British Museum, one at Lincoln Castle, and one is on display in the Chapter House in Salisbury Cathedral. It runs to about 3,500 words.

HENRY III

Reigned 1216-1272

Born 1.10.1207 in Winchester

Died 16.11.1272 in Winchester

Son of King John and Isabella of Angoulême

Married Eleanor of Provence

Four sons and two daughters

In many ways Henry was quite untypical of kings in those years. He was the first peaceful and arts-loving king since Edward the Confessor, and recognised this similarity himself, spending much of his time enlarging and beautifying Westminster Abbey in order to give greater honour to the Confessor.

He was nine when he was crowned, and so obviously there had to be guardians and regents. It is probably true to say that Henry never did quite learn to take control of things. He was far too interested in his building projects, and also far too generous to his many French relations.

His wife, Eleanor of Provence, certainly brought culture to England, but she also brought a huge retinue of foreign friends and relations.

Henry was kind. Too kind. He gave away so much, and spent so much on his artistic projects that eventually the barons rebelled at the costly way he was ruling. When Henry asked for yet more money, he was forced to sign a set of guide-lines called the Provisions of Oxford, in which he had to submit to a form of Parliament, summoned by a capable ring-leader among the barons, Simon de Montfort, Earl of Leicester.

Two things emerged from Henry's reign: the beginnings of Parliament, and the beautifully rebuilt Westminster Abbey. In a way, they represented two very positive marks of progress. Many cathedrals were built or rebuilt in his time, with his encouragement: Wells, Lincoln, Peterborough, Salisbury. The Great Hall in Winchester where visitors today can see 'King Arthur's Table' was built by him.

Franciscan and Dominican friars came to England during his reign, and the universities of Oxford and Cambridge were beginning to establish themselves. England was gradually becoming civilised.

Henry is buried, appropriately, near his beloved Edward the Confessor in the enlarged Westminster Abbey which is his greatest memorial.

EDWARD I

Reigned 1272-1307

Born 17.6.1239 in Westminster
Died 7.7.1307 at Burgh-by-Sands, Carlisle
Son of Henry III and Eleanor of Provence

Married (i) Eleanor of Castile
(ii) Margaret of France
Three sons and five daughters by Eleanor
and two sons and one daughter by Margaret

Like so many successful monarchs, Edward possessed intense energy, ferocious fighting skills, and supreme determination. However to these qualities he added the essential virtue of a good ruler – he genuinely wanted to bring law, order and prosperity to the land. He saw what was wanted, took good advice, and recognised that his first duty was to his country rather than to himself.

We owe the British Parliament to Edward. He organised what was called the Model Parliament in 1295, laying down the system of representative government which we have developed over the centuries. In this, his ideas were well before the times he lived in.

Also we owe much of our legal system to his inspiration: the great common law courts took shape under his active encouragement.

He tried harder than any king before him to create a United Kingdom, and almost succeeded. He created the title of 'Prince of Wales' as he presented his newborn son as a kind of peace-offering to the Welsh. However, Scotland was a failure. He made three attempts to subdue Scotland, but none was decisive. In the first he defeated John Balliol; in the second he defeated William Wallace; and when Robert the Bruce had himself crowned King of Scotland, taking William Wallace's place, Edward planned a third attempt.

By now Edward was getting on for seventy, still in the saddle, still determined to press on with what he saw as an essential unifying task. He got as far as Burgh-by-Sands, near Carlisle, and then fell ill and died.

We have no picture or effigy of this great king. His tomb in Westminster Abbey is a vast ugly lump with the famous inscription 'Hammer of the Scots' scrawled on its side – a bit of 17th century graffiti on a 14th century stone coffin.

EDWARD II

Reigned 1307-1327

Born 25.4.1284 in Caernarvon Castle
Died 21.9.1327 in Berkeley Castle
Son of Edward I and Eleanor of Castile
Married Isabella of France
Two sons, two daughters

It has been said that Edward II was his father's greatest failure.

He was only 23 when he succeeded Edward I. A greater contrast could hardly be imagined between the two sovereigns.

It was plain to his wife, Princess Isabella of France, and to everyone else that his sexual appetites were centred on the insufferably vain and grasping Piers Gaveston. As soon as she arrived in England, aged 12, to marry Edward, Isabella noticed that Gaveston was wearing rings and jewels which her own father had just given to Edward. And Edward and his gay companion were publicly kissing and embracing.

The barons finally could not put up with Gaveston. They trapped him and cut off his head. It was then that Edward turned his homosexual affections to the Despensers, father and son.

During this disastrous reign Scotland finally asserted its independence by inflicting a resounding defeat upon Edward at the Battle of Bannockburn, 1314.

Isabella's patience finally gave way. She took a lover, Roger Mortimer, and together they led rebellions against Edward.

Edward was forced to abdicate and was imprisoned in Berkeley Castle. He suffered the cruellest fate to befall any English monarch: he was murdered by having a red-hot poker thrust up his anus.

EDWARD II AND GLOUCESTER CATHEDRAL

The horrific murder of Edward II had one positive benefit – the redecoration of Gloucester cathedral, where he was buried. Edward's son, King Edward III, gave his father a superbly beautiful tomb there, which became a shrine for thousands of sight-seeing pilgrims.

As a result, the cathedral became richer and richer; the monks planned more and more magnificent additions and alterations; and Gloucester cathedral ushered in a unique new style of architecture – known today as the Perpendicular Style.

EDWARD III

Reigned 1327-1377

Born 13.11.1312 in Windsor Castle
Died 21.6.1377 in Sheen Palace, Surrey
Son of Edward II and Isabella of France
Married Philippa of Hainault
Six sons, five daughters

Edward was only aged 14 when he became king, and swiftly seized real power, personally capturing his mother and her lover, Roger Mortimer, as they shared a bedroom in Nottingham Castle. After a show trial, Mortimer was executed and Isabella, though pardoned, was put under virtual house-arrest for the rest of her life.

Edward was the archetypal mediaeval kingly king. Tall, handsome, magnificently generous, filled with noble ideas of grandeur. He entertained on a grand scale. He won resounding victories over the French both on sea (Battle of Sluys, 1340) and land (Battle of Crécy, 1346); gained huge tracts of territory; treated captured kings (David of Scotland and John of France) as honoured guests.

His son and heir, the Black Prince, also won a tremendous victory over the French at Poitiers (1356). He built a splendid shrine in Gloucester cathedral in memory of his dead father. It seemed that whatever he did was effected with honour, success and more than a touch of royal glamour.

He swore to establish a new order of Arthurian knights, and at a ball to celebrate the capture of Calais the garter of one of the court ladies fell to the floor. With a dramatic royal gesture, Edward immediately picked it up and tied it round his own leg. His famous remark as he did so, "Honi soit qui mal y pense" ("Evil be to him who evil thinks") is still the proud motto of the Garter Knights, for this was the occasion when he fulfilled his vow to create his company of noble knights. The Garter Chapel at Windsor continues to give a thrill of historical greatness even today.

Alas, as he grew older, many of his triumphs turned sour. The French gradually regained much of the land he gained; the Black Death brought economic disasters; the heir to the throne, the famous Black Prince, died in mid-life; and Edward himself became prematurely senile and a victim of his greedy mistress, Alice Perrers, who stripped him of his jewels even as he lay on his death-bed.

He had been a great king, and his regal effigy in Westminster Abbey seems almost too perfect: aloof and God-like.

RICHARD II

Reigned 1377-1399

Born 6.1.1367 in Bordeaux, France
Died 14.2.1400 in Pontefract Castle
Son of Edward the Black Prince and Joan of Kent
Grandson of Edward III
Married (i) Anne of Bohemia
(ii) Isabella of France
No children

When a child comes to the throne it is almost always a recipe for disaster, and Richard was only ten when he was crowned.

There were plenty of ambitious uncles to tell him what to do, and as Richard grew into adulthood he resented this more and more.

As a boy of fourteen he had shown much courage in defusing an ugly situation during the Peasants' Revolt of 1381, when there was a demonstration against the Poll Tax. A mob had gathered and the Mayor of London had just stabbed and killed their leader, Wat Tyler. Richard boldly rode up to the crowd alone and persuaded them to disperse quietly. It was his finest hour.

However, his reign was flamboyant and extravagant. He and his first wife, Anne of Bohemia wore quite extraordinary clothes, ate exotic dishes, and were passionately interested in literature, fashion and the arts.

His lasting achievement was the rebuilding of Westminster Hall with its magnificent hammer-beam roof; and he also gave generously towards York Minster, Canterbury Cathedral, and the royal residences at Eltham and Sheen.

His wife, Anne, died childless, aged only 28, and Richard was devastated. He ordered the palace of Sheen, where she died, to be completely demolished and razed to the ground. And as the country needed an heir he married again, an extraordinary choice – a little eight-year-old French Princess.

His reign became more and more arbitrary, and eventually his cousin Henry Bolingbroke led an open rebellion, forced Richard to abdicate and proclaimed himself Henry IV.

Within a few months Richard was dead. No one will ever know exactly what the circumstances were, but Shakespeare gives a memorable account of a possible murder.

HENRY IV

Reigned 1399-1413

Born April 1366 in Bolingbroke Castle, Lincs
Died 20.3.1413 in Westminster
Son of John of Gaunt and Blanche of Lancaster
Grandson of Edward III
Married (i) Mary de Bohun
Married (ii) Joan of Navarre (sometimes known as Joan of Brittany)
Four sons and three daughters by Mary

Henry Bolingbroke, as he was born, was only a few months older than his cousin, Richard II, and there was no love lost between them.

Henry had been one of the 'Lords Appellant' – a council of five noblemen set up to help rule the country during Richard II's minority.

As soon as he could, Richard disbanded these Lords Appellant, beheaded two of them and imprisoned a third; the other two were Henry Bolingbroke and the Duke of Norfolk. When these two fell out with one another Richard staged a duel between them, and then at the last moment stepped in and forbade it, banishing Norfolk for life and Bolingbroke for ten years.

Dutifully, Bolingbroke went abroad, but when his father died Richard seized all his (Bolingbroke's) rightful inheritance. Quite naturally Bolingbroke was filled with anger and vengeance, and returned home to claim his rights.

Bolingbroke's revenge took the form of seizing Richard and then the throne. He set himself up as King Henry IV, arranged for Richard to be murdered, and then tried to prove that he had a legal right to the succession.

This 'scrambling and unquiet time' as Shakespeare called it led to a constant succession of rebellions. There were constant troubles: arguments in parliament, fighting along the Welsh and Scottish borders, plots and skirmishes. Executions were constantly necessary, simply to keep himself in power. Henry even executed the Archbishop of York, who had supported one of the rebellions.

Henry, then, was a usurper. He had a bad conscience about having seized the throne and the strain of maintaining his position undermined his health. He died in a kind of fit as he was praying in Westminster Abbey, in the 'Jerusalem Chamber' which is alongside the present bookshop outside the Abbey. Curiously enough, an astrologer had predicted that he would die 'in Jerusalem', and Henry had been planning to go there, perhaps on a crusade to heal his guilt.

He is buried in Canterbury Cathedral.

HENRY V

Reigned 1413-1422

Born 9.8.1387 or 16.9.1387 in Monmouth, Wales

Died 31.8.1422 in Vincennes Castle, France

Son of Henry IV and Mary de Bohun

Married Catherine of Valois

One son

Shakespeare has given us a picture of a charismatic young leader who led a riotous youth and then became an outstanding soldier-king. Allowing for poetic licence, this is true.

Henry V was a superb soldier and leader of men. His outstanding victory at Agincourt, 1415, seized the imagination of the country. His army of 8,000 suffered negligible losses, yet the opposing French army of 50,000 was totally crushed with thousands of men killed or taken prisoner.

Henry's rapturous welcome home after Agincourt was unlike anything seen before. Literally, wine ran from public fountains.

His marriage to Catherine of Valois was both political and romantic. He not only gained a huge dowry and became heir to the French throne, but also gained a beautiful and loving wife.

But his success was brief. War with France never ceased. He was constantly trying to gain more and more territory, conquering and avenging. Two years after his marriage, still with his army, he caught dysentery and died.

His little son and heir, another Henry, was just nine months old.

LONDON MOURNS FOR THE HERO OF AGINCOURT

The death of Henry V brought consternation to London. As the funeral procession entered the capital every citizen, rich or poor, stood on his doorstep with a lighted taper. A first requiem was sung at Old St. Paul's, and then a magnificent ceremony was held in Westminster Abbey.

Henry's V's three chargers, draped with black velvet blazoned with the arms of England and France, were led by mailed knights up the nave into the choir, and stood motionless throughout the service.

Henry was then laid to rest in the most sacred part of the Abbey – the Chapel of Edward the Confessor. His 21-year-old widow, Catherine, ordered a special chantry chapel to be built there, in the shape of an H.

HENRY VI

Reigned 1422-1461 and 1470-1471

Born 6.12.1421 in Windsor Castle
Died 21st May, 1471, in the Tower of London
Son of Henry V and Catherine of Valois
Married Margaret of Anjou
One son

This gentle, scholarly and religious man was temperamentally simply not suited to be king. He would much rather have been a monk. But it was his misfortune to succeed to the throne when he was only nine months old.

Naturally, there were plenty of nobles who were only too anxious to take over power and throughout his reign he was for all practical purposes regarded as a puppet. The Yorkist and Lancastrian rivals in the Wars of the Roses battled away over his head. Sometimes he was king. Sometimes he wasn't.

The situation was made worse by the fact that twice in his life he suffered a complete mental breakdown. The first lasted for about eighteen months, and when he recovered he was 'as a man who wakes after a long dream'. He had to be introduced to his own baby son, who had been born during his loss of consciousness.

Eventually he was deposed and murdered in the Tower of London.

Despite his unworldliness and ineffectiveness as a king, Henry was a passionate lover of religion and education. He immersed himself in establishing the two outstandingly beautiful educational foundations, Eton College near Windsor and King's College Cambridge. These are his permanent memorials.

Visitors to the Tower of London can see a plaque on a floor in the Wakefield Tower, marking the spot where Henry was murdered.

SAINT HENRY?

After his murder, Henry was buried deliberately in a rather out-of-the way place, Chertsey Abbey in Surrey. But such was his popular esteem that it was claimed that no fewer than 174 miracles took place at his tomb.

Richard III had his body transferred and reburied in St. George's Chapel, Windsor, where his tomb attracted large numbers of pilgrims. Henry VII was determined to support a move to make Henry a saint, but he died before this could be accomplished. Henry VIII's break with Rome finally destroyed the negotiation procedures. Even today there are still people who would like to see this unfortunate king canonised as a saint.

EDWARD IV

Reigned 1461-1470 and 1471-1483

Born 28.4.1422 in Rouen, France

Died 9.4.1483 in Westminster

Son of Richard, 3rd Duke of York and Cicely, daughter of the 1st Earl of Westmoreland

Married Elizabeth Woodville

Two sons and seven daughters

The weakness and mental instability of Henry VI inevitably led to a power struggle. Edward, a distant cousin of Henry VI, took full advantage of the situation. He was aware that Henry's grandfather had usurped the throne, so he felt no pangs of conscience about usurping the throne for himself.

Henry VI was a member of the House of Lancaster, descended from John of Gaunt, Duke of Lancaster; Edward IV was a member of the House of York, descended from John of Gaunt's younger brother, Edmund, Duke of York. This is the background of the 'Wars of the Roses' in which the Yorkists and Lancastrians struggled for supremacy: descendants of two brothers.

Lancastrians had a red rose as their emblem: Yorkists had a white rose. Ultimately, the Tudors united these colours in the red and white 'Tudor Rose', symbolising reconciliation.

Although the Lancastrians managed to gain victories at Wakefield (1460) and St Albans (1461), the Yorkists were generally much better organised, and Edward gained the throne at the bloodiest battle in English history, fought in snow just outside the Yorkshire town of Towton, in 1461.

Henry VI and Edward IV each had two periods of kingship, but after the decisive Battle of Tewkesbury (1471) Edward finally won, murdered Henry and remained king until his death twelve years later.

After a life of battles to gain the English throne, Edward then invaded France. With success at the Treaty of Picquigny in 1475 he squeezed 75,000 crowns out of the French King Louis XI plus annual payments of 20,000 if only he would leave France for good. It was virtually a protection racket, and Edward lived comfortably until his sudden death, aged only 41.

Edward encouraged the new invention of printing, helping William Caxton to set up printing-presses in Westminster. He also built one of England's greatest architectural glories – St George's Chapel, Windsor. He himself was the first king to be buried there. His gigantic sword still hangs beside the spot where he lies.

EDWARD V

'Reigned' 9th April to 25th June 1483

Born 2.11.1470 in Westminster

Died September 1483 in the Tower of London

Son of Edward IV and Elizabeth Woodville

One of the 'Princes In the Tower', probably murdered on the orders of his uncle King Richard III a few weeks before his thirteenth birthday.

The fate of the 'Princes in the Tower' is virtually a part of English folklore, but few people can remember exactly who these 'Princes' were.

The fact is, one of them was King Edward V, aged 12, who was never crowned. He was regarded as king from the moment his father Edward IV suddenly and unexpectedly died of pneumonia. The other Prince was Richard, Duke of York, his brother aged 9 and heir to the throne.

Anyone else who wanted to become king therefore would have to do away with both of these boys. The finger of history points accusingly at their uncle, Richard, Duke of Gloucester. He proclaimed himself King Richard III, and as for the royal children, prisoners in the Tower of London, they simply disappeared.

Some human bones were discovered in the Tower about two centuries later, and Charles II ordered them to be interred in Westminster Abbey.

KING ARTHUR

Much has been written about King Arthur, but even his most enthusiastic admirers must admit that they know almost nothing about him.

A legendary history of Arthur was written in about 1135 by Geoffrey of Monmouth; Sir Thomas Malory wrote his prose romance 'Morte d'Arthur' in the late fifteenth century; and Lord Tennyson wrote his 'Idylls of the King' in the middle of the nineteenth century .

If Arthur existed at all, he was a British (i.e.Celtic) leader in the West of England, fighting against the invading Saxons, possibly around the year 500 AD.

He is supposed to have fought a series of stupendous battles, beginning at 'Mount Badon', which may have been Bath, and finishing with a defeat at 'Camlann' (perhaps Cadbury Castle, in Somserset) where he was wounded. His death is not described. We are left with an image of Arthur being taken away to 'Avalon' (perhaps Glastonbury) to be healed.

According to Geoffrey of Monmouth, Arthur was born at Tintagel in Cornwall and is buried at Glastonbury.

There are many places in Wales and in the West of England which are also linked in legend with Arthur, and a famous 'Round Table' is hung in a mediaeval hall in Winchester, decorated with pictures of his Knights.

The stories are compelling, but they are, alas, only stories . . .

RICHARD III

Reigned 1483-1485

Born 2.10.1452 in Fotheringhay Castle, Northants

Died 22.8.1485 at the Battle of Bosworth, near Leicester

Son of Richard, Third Duke of York, and Lady Cecily Neville

Married Anne Neville

One son

Shakespeare has given us an unforgettable picture of Richard III as a villainous hunchback, but then, Shakespeare lived in the reign of Queen Elizabeth, whose grandfather, Henry VII, had won the battle of Bosworth, witnessed the death of Richard and had seized the crown.

Richard succeeded his brother Edward IV, who died suddenly of pneumonia. and is generally believed to have murdered his way to the throne, by eliminating the two young princes ('The Princes in the Tower') who were the legitimate heirs to the crown. Circumstantial evidence strongly points to this, however nothing can be proved.

Richard had hardly time to do much in a short reign of only twenty-six months. He was popular in the north, but like all usurpers he had many enemies, and had to deal with a rebellion led by his former friend and ally, the Duke of Buckingham.

Buckingham was beheaded in Salisbury market-place and Richard knew that from then on his enemies were looking towards Henry Tudor, Earl of Richmond, as a new leader.

Henry bided his time in Britanny, then crossed to Milford Haven, hoping to gain Welshmen for his cause. Then he marched towards Leicester where the decisive Battle of Bosworth brought the long succession of Plantagenets to an end. Richard was killed and his bones were flung into a river and lost. The Tudors had taken over.

WICKED MONSTER OR INNOCENT VICTIM OF SLANDER?

Virtually all Tudor writers elaborated Richard's ugliness and evil character. It was given out that he had spent two years in his mother's womb, and after a difficult birth he had emerged with hair down to his shoulders and a full set of teeth – "To signify thou cam'st to bite the world . . ."

No contemporary picture exists of Richard, so in the face of all the bad press given him by the Tudors, it is impossible to arrive at the truth.

HENRY VII

Reigned 1485-1509

Born 28.1.1457 in Pembroke Castle, Wales

Died 21/4/1509 in Richmond Palace, Surrey

Son of Edmund, 1st Earl of Richmond and Margaret Beaufort

Married Elizabeth of York, daughter of Edward IV

Two sons and two daughters

After the troubles of the Wars of the Roses England desperately needed a period of stability. It was Henry's sheer mastery of statecraft which helped steer the country back into peace and prosperity. He may perhaps appear somewhat dull as a king, but he had had excitement enough as a young man and was wise enough to realise that kingship was a skill which needed hard and patient work.

He dealt with two possible threats from people pretending to have claims to the throne: Lambert Simnel and Perkin Warbeck, treating both of these with leniency, refusing to make martyrs out of them.

His marriage to Edward IV's daughter, Elizabeth of York, successfully united the warring factions of York and Lancaster. The red and white 'Tudor Rose' was a logo which everybody could understand: unity at last.

We owe much to Henry VII. He gave England stability and prosperity, which it desperately needed; he founded the remarkable Tudor dynasty; he started England off on its course of exploration and foreign trade in the newly discovered world, encouraging the Cabots in their voyages to North America.

Finally, we must thank him for one of the most beautiful pieces of architecture in the world – his chapel in Westminster Abbey. His other architectural masterpiece, Richmond Palace, has not survived.

Henry died relatively young, aged 52, saddened by the death of his first son, Arthur, on whom he had placed much hope, and by the death of his wife Elizabeth. But in his reign England had made the turning-point from the middle ages to modern times.

THE YEOMEN OF THE GUARD

The 'Beefeaters' or Yeomen of the Guard were first formed by Henry VII as a royal bodyguard for his coronation in 1485. The name 'Beefeater' also refers to the Yeomen Extraordinary of the Guard, formed by Edward VI as Warders of the Tower of London, and who wear the same uniform.

Henry VII had the uniform specially designed, and it is largely retained to this day.

WHERE KINGS ARE BURIED

Edward the Confessor	Westminster Abbey
William the Conqueror	St. Stephen's Abbey, Caen
William II ('Rufus')	Winchester Cathedral
Henry I	Reading Abbey (now destroyed)
Stephen	Faversham Abbey (now destroyed)
Henry II	Fontevrault Abbey, France
Richard I	Fontevrault Abbey, France
John	Worcester Cathedral
Henry III	Westminster Abbey
Edward I	Westminster Abbey
Edward II	Gloucester Cathedral
Edward III	Westminster Abbey
Richard II	Westminster Abbey
Henry IV	Canterbury Cathedral
Henry V	Westminster Abbey
Henry VI	St. George's Chapel, Windsor
Edward IV	St. George's Chapel, Windsor
Edward V	Unknown: possibly Westminster Abbey
Richard III	Unknown: bones thrown away
Henry VII	Westminster Abbey
Henry VIII	St. George's Chapel, Windsor
Edward VI	Westminster Abbey
Jane Grey	Chapel in the Tower of London
Mary I	Westminster Abbey
Elizabeth I	Westminster Abbey
James I	Westminster Abbey
Charles I	St. George's Chapel, Windsor
Charles II	Westminster Abbey
James II	St. Germain-en-Laye, near Paris
William III and Mary II	Both in Westminster Abbey
Anne	Westminster Abbey
George I	Herrenhausen, Hanover
George II	Westminster Abbey
George III	St. George's Chapel, Windsor
George IV	St. George's Chapel, Windsor
William IV	St. George's Chapel, Windsor
Victoria	Royal Mausoleum, Frogmore, Windsor
Edward VII	St. George's Chapel, Windsor
George V	St. George's Chapel, Windsor
Edward VIII	Royal Burial Ground, Frogmore, Windsor
George VI	St. George's Chapel, Windsor

HENRY VIII

Reigned 1509-1547

Born 28.6.1491 at Greenwich Palace

Died 28.1.1547 St. James's Palace, London

Son of Henry VII and Elizabeth of York

Married (i) Catherine of Aragon (divorced 1533)
(ii) Anne Boleyn (beheaded 1536)
(iii) Jane Seymour (died 1537)
(iv) Anne of Cleves (divorced 1540)
(v) Catherine Howard (beheaded 1542)
(vi) Catherine Parr (survived Henry by four years)

One son, the future Edward VI, by Jane Seymour
a daughter, the future Queen Mary, by Catherine of Aragon
and a daughter, the future Queen Elizabeth I, by Anne Boleyn

Henry VIII began life as a talented, attractive and intelligent man, but became increasingly cruel, ruthless and dictatorial. However he was popular throughout his reign, and even today the cocksure figure of 'Bluff King Hal' has a quaint and comforting charm about it.

He was not quite 18 when he came to the throne and just a few days before his coronation he had married a Spanish Princess, Catherine of Aragon. She was 24 at the time and had previously been the wife of Henry's older brother, Arthur.

Arthur had died suddenly in 1502, so in a sense Henry inherited both wife and throne.

The troubles of the Wars of the Roses were only a generation away, and the Tudors were still considered upstarts by many of the old Plantagenet supporters. Therefore it was vital that Henry should have a son and heir. A nightmare of chaos was likely unless there was a clear succession.

As the years went on Catherine of Aragon seemed less and less likely to produce the necessary son. True, they had a girl, Mary, but that wasn't quite enough. Thus began the long and tragic succession of marriage disasters that marked Henry's reign.

After more than twenty years with Catherine of Aragon, Henry fell in love with the 'concubine' Anne Boleyn. She stuck out for marriage, so Henry did everything he could to get a divorce. He broke with the Catholic Church of Rome and made himself head of the English church. In the process he abolished ('dissolved') all the monasteries in the country.

Anne Boleyn enjoyed a brief 3-year marriage, but was beheaded for alleged infidelity. Her fate was not helped by the fact that she too did not produce a son. Their only daughter, Elizabeth, was declared a bastard.

Henry's next wife, Jane Seymour, was more successful. She did produce a son, Edward, but she died within a few days.

Thomas Cromwell, Henry's chief adviser at the time, suggested Anne of Cleves as the next wife, for political reasons. Although Holbein produced a favourable picture of her, Henry was disgusted by Anne's looks. He went through a marriage ceremony but quickly divorced her. Cromwell was beheaded.

Meanwhile he had fallen in love again, this time with Catherine Howard, a lively 20-year-old. But she was too lively, and after eighteen months he had her beheaded for alleged adultery.

His last wife, Catherine Parr, survived him, nursing him in the last years of his life. Even she almost lost her head for voicing her religious opinions too freely.

Henry's marriages make fascinating reading and they are what most people remember. However his real contribution to England's history lies in the gigantic religious and social changes he made. Breaking the power of the Catholic church in England and dissolving all 823 abbeys and monasteries was by far the most far-reaching change in the whole life-style of the country. Thomas Cromwell pushed through these changes with incredible ruthlessness. Within a few years hundreds of beautiful buildings were broken up and all the monks were forced to abandon their monastic ways.

On the credit side, Henry vastly strengthened the English navy; personally supervised the completion of the magnificent extension to Westminster Abbey known as Henry VII's Chapel; added to the great palace of Hampton Court, given to him by Cardinal Wolsey; and he founded Trinity College Cambridge.

It was an immensely energetic reign. He incorporated Wales into England; made Ireland a kingdom; waged wars in France and Scotland; and involved himself deeply in the religious controversies of the time – ironically defending the Catholic church against Protestantism, despite his break with Rome.

Above all, Henry tolerated no opposition. He executed at least 50 people who crossed his will, including his three powerful chief advisers, Cardinal Wolsey, Sir Thomas More, and Thomas Cromwell.

Henry is buried in St George's Chapel, Windsor, but has no memorial.

EDWARD VI

Reigned 1547-1553

Born 12.10.1537 at Hampton Court Palace
Died 6.7.1553 in Greenwich Palace
Son of Henry VIII and Jane Seymour

A precocious and rather cold child. He was only nine years old when he came to the throne and was fifteen when he died.

In the early years of his reign he was guided by his mother's brother, Edward Seymour, Duke of Somerset, who took the title of Lord Protector. But when he was twelve there was a power-struggle and the role of Protector was taken over by Robert Dudley, Duke of Northumberland. Somerset was executed.

Edward was highly intelligent, taking a keen interest in all the religious controversies of the age. He was a fanatical supporter of the new Protestantism. He liked nothing better than to argue theological issues with bishops: among his Court Preachers were John Knox and Bishops Ridley, Cranmer, Latimer and Hooper.

In mediaeval England people left sums of money to have masses said for them after their death. In large churches and cathedrals there are beautiful 'Chantries' where these masses used to be said. Protestants, however, no longer believed in saying prayers for the dead, and a special Act of Parliament, the 'Dissolution of the Chantries Act' put a final stop to this ancient custom.

Many of the chantry priests had been useful in providing local education, so when education seemed to suffer as a result of this Act, Edward was personally concerned to establish new grammar schools to make up this loss. To this day there are a number of 'King Edward VI' schools in England, dating from this time.

Poor Edward. He caught consumpton and spent many months dying. Plans to marry him off to all sorts of people had to be abandoned. His 'Protector', the Duke of Northumberland, did not publicly declare Edward's death for several days, so that he could make schemes for the succession. There were even rumours of poison.

Edward would have been horrified if he knew that his Catholic half-sister Mary would succeed him.

"Oh my Lord God, defend this realm from papistry," were his last words.

He suffered poor health and died of tuberculosis. He is buried in Westminster Abbey.

LADY JANE GREY

Reigned for nine days in July 1553

Born September 1537 in Bradgate Park, Leicester

Died 12.2.1554 in the Tower of London

Daughter of Henry Grey, 3rd Marquess of Dorset and Lady Frances Brandon

There is no more pathetic figure in the whole line of British kings and queens than Lady Jane Grey, who was only fifteen when she became queen, and sixteen when she was beheaded.

She spent her life among royalty, being a great grand-daughter of King Henry VII. If King Edward VI had lived, it was quite likely that she might have married him.

Her fate was to become a pawn in a protestant plot to prevent Henry VIII's Catholic daughter Mary from coming to the throne. It was the idea of the Earl of Northumberland, the 'Protector' of Edward VI. He schemed to put Lady Jane on the throne, marry her to his son who would then become king, so that he himself would still remain the power behind the monarchy.

The tragedy of Jane was that she knew clearly from the beginning that she was being wrongly used; she did not in the least want to become queen; yet despite her protests she was bullied into submission. So, without being crowned, she was proclaimed 'Queen' and remained so for nine days.

Mary, of course, quickly claimed the throne. The Duke of Northumberland was executed immediately. Jane was kept prisoner in the Tower of London for six months before Mary finally decided to have her executed too.

From her room in the Tower she saw the decapitated body of her teenage husband Guilford Dudley trundled past her apartments in a handcart, knowing that within minutes it would be her turn to lay her head on the block.

As she stood on Tower Green that cold February morning she made a brave speech, saying "I do wash my hands in innocency before God."

But the axeman was ready. "So perish all the Queen's enemies!" he declared as he held up a hideous dripping object. "Behold the head of a traitor!"

Her body lies in the crypt of the chapel of St Peter ad Vincula in the Tower of London.

MARY I

Reigned 1553-1558

Born 8.2.1516 in Greenwich Palace

Died 17.11.1558 in St. James's Palace, London

Daughter of Henry VIII and Catherine of Aragon

Married Prince Philip of Spain

No children

Mary had endured a terrible childhood. Her mother, Catherine of Aragon, had been rejected and banished from court; she herself was publicly declared a bastard; she lived through all the tumult of her Henry's later marriages; and as a fervent Catholic she saw her father dismantle the whole structure of the Catholic church in England.

Then, she had witnessed her precocious little half-brother, Edward, 21 years younger than herself, menacing in his insistence that she should abandon her Catholic religion and follow his own Protestantism. And finally, when he died, she had to manoeuvre her way through the inept plot to put Lady Jane Grey on the throne instead of herself.

When eventually, aged 37, she became queen, she was ruthlessly determined to restore the Catholic faith to England, come what may.

She was anxious to marry and if possible provide England with an heir, and her choice fell unhappily on Prince Philip of Spain. They were married in Winchester Cathedral, and he became King of England in title, though without power. He barely concealed his dislike of her, and left England within months.

Pathetically, Mary thought she was pregnant, but her swollen stomach turned out to be the symptom of some dreadful illness. She was heartbroken to find out that she had deluded herself by imagining a pregnancy.

Meanwhile, determined as ever to rid the realm of Protestants, she literally and physically burnt hundreds of people all over the country who still clung to their Protestant faith. They ranged from bishops and even a former archbishop (Cranmer) to ordinary humble folk, weavers, shoemakers, wheelwrights. Even cripples and blind youngsters were pushed into the flames.

No one ever forgot or forgave. Even in her lifetime she was called 'Bloody Mary'.

Joining Spain in a war against France, she was responsible for the loss of Calais. It was the final piece of French territory to be lost – breaking the link with France which had begun with William the Conqueror.

She is buried in Westminster Abbey, given the last Roman Catholic burial to take place there.

'BLOODY MARY' AND THE VICTIMS OF RELIGIOUS PERSECUTION

Statistics are notoriously unreliable, but according to one account the number of people burnt during the reign of Mary amounted to 288, and many more perished in prison, starved or maltreated. The burnings are well authenticated, and left terrible memories of her reign.

An edition of Foxe's Book of Martyrs, giving details, records: "There were burnt 5 bishops, 21 divines, 8 gentlemen, 84 artificers, 100 husbandmen, servants and labourers, 25 wives, 9 virgins, 2 boys and 2 infants. 64 more were persecuted for the religion, whereof 7 were whipped, 16 perished in prison and 12 were buried in dunghills."

The deaths took place all over the country, in the four years from 1555 to 1558. The first recorded was John Rogers, a priest, who was burnt at Smithfield in London on 4 February, 1555, and the last were John Corneford, Christopher Browne, John Herst, Alice Snoth and Catherine Tynley, all of whom were burnt at Canterbury on 10 November, 1558, just a week before Mary herself died.

It is only when we remember the scale of this terror that we can understand the desperate reluctance to bring back another Catholic monarch to the throne. Shouts of "No Popery" have been heard even in the 20th century.

Here are just twelve typical entries from a list given in a 19th century edition of Foxe's Book of Martyrs: (the full list runs into hundreds).

William Andrew	carpenter	Newgate	August 1555	Died in prison
John Newman	pewterer	Saffron Walden	Aug. 31 1555	Burnt
Thomas Cob	butcher	Thetford	Sept. 1555	Burnt
William Wolsey	constable	Ely	Oct 1555	Burnt
Dr. Nicholas Ridley	Bishop	Oxford	Oct 16 1555	Burnt
Dr. Hugh Latimer	Bishop	Oxford	Oct 16 1555	Burnt
John Fortune	blacksmith	Norwich	June 1556	Died in prison
Joan Waste	a blind girl	Derby	Aug 1 1556	Burnt
John Archer	weaver	Canterbury Castle	Nov 1557	Famished
Elizabeth	a blind girl	Maidstone	June 18 1557	Burnt
Barbara Final	widow	Canterbury	June 30 1557	Burnt
Thomas Benbridge	gentleman	Smithfield	July 1558	Burnt

ELIZABETH I

Reigned 1558-1603

Born 7.9.1533 in Greenwich Palace

Died 24.3.1603 in Richmond Palace, Surrey

Daughter of Henry VIII and Anne Boleyn

Unmarried

Without doubt, Elizabeth was one of the world's greatest monarchs. She dominated England for almost half a century and has fascinated historians ever since.

The secret of her brilliant skill in statecraft probably lies in the terrible events she experienced during those dangerous twenty-five years before she became queen.

She was only $2^1/_2$ when her mother, Queen Anne Boleyn, was beheaded. She lived to see four step-mothers disappear: one dying after childbirth, the next divorced, the next beheaded, and the final one, Catherine Parr, dying in childbirth having remarried after the death of Henry VIII. She was publicly declared a bastard, and knew what it was to be poor, unloved and virtually under constant house-arrest.

Perhaps her worst moment was during the reign of her half-sister Mary, when she was taken, aged 20, as prisoner to the Tower of London, suspected of treason. Life must have seemed absolutely hopeless. At first she refused to enter the Tower by the 'Traitors' Gate' and sat weeping on a stone by the muddy river-bank. "I am come in no traitor," she sobbed, "but as a true woman to the Queen's majesty."

But they forced her in and she remained prisoner for two months.

All through these desperate years she learned many lessons. She learned how to survive. She learned how to be diplomatic. And, seeing the mistakes of others, she learned how to be Queen.

So when Mary died, Elizabeth took to her duties with consummate artistry. No one has ever practised royal skills so successfully.

She dressed with spectacular finery and delighted in moving about the country, staying with loyal and enthusiastic subjects. The people loved her and she flattered them as no other monarch has ever done before or since, by telling them how much she loved them. "You may well have a greater prince," she said, "but you shall never have a more loving prince".

One notable feature of her reign was the calming-down of religious fanaticism. Feelings were still high after the intolerance of the previous reigns. But Elizabeth's protestantism was less ferocious.

Nevertheless, possible threats against the throne were another matter. Elizabeth felt she simply had to order the execution of her Catholic cousin, Mary Queen of Scots. But it took her months to bring herself to sign the death-warrant.

All through her reign she used her virginity to tease and intrigue. Marriage was a trump-card which she constantly had in her hand, but which she resolutely refused to play. Who would she marry? Philip of Spain? The Duke of Alençon? The Archduke of Austria? No one could tell. Her heart probably belonged to Robert Dudley, Earl of Leicester, but somehow the years slipped by and to the end she remained the Virgin Queen.

She was pleased when Sir Walter Raleigh proposed calling his new American settlement 'Virginia' after her. It's probably the only territory ever named after spinsterhood!

Her long reign was remarkable for great men and great events: Shakespeare, Francis Drake, Walter Raleigh, Philip Sidney. She remained at the centre of events and caught the spirit of the age. 'Elizabethan England', especially after the defeat of the Spanish Armada in 1588, still brings to mind in many people's minds the picture of a Golden Age.

As never before, it was an age of great literature, grand architecture, exciting discoveries and daring exploration.

Here is a part of her magnificent speech at Tilbury, when she talked directly to her troops, inspiring courage in the face of threatened invasion. Who could resist these words?

> *"Let tyrants fear . . . I have placed my chiefest strength and goodwill in the loyal hearts and goodwill of my subjects . . . I know I have but the body of a weak and feeble woman: but I have the heart and stomach of a king – and a king of England too – and I think it foul scorn that Parma or Spain or any Prince of Europe should dare to invade the borders of my realm."*

Surely this remains the greatest speech ever made by an English monarch.

Her magnificent tomb in Westminster Abbey shows her in old age. It does not flatter: even today we can sense the awe she must have inspired.

JAMES I

Reigned as James VI of Scotland 1567-1625
Reigned as James I of England 1603-1625

Born 19.6.1566 in Edinburgh Castle

Died 27.3.1625 in Theobalds Park, Hertfordshire

Son of Mary, Queen of Scots and Henry Stuart, Lord Darnley

Married Anne of Denmark

Three sons and four daughters

James had been a king since babyhood, but was 37 when he moved from his modest Edinburgh court to the elaborate sophistication of London. He was something of an eccentric; it has been said that he was made up of two men: a nervous drivelling idiot, and a witty, well-read scholar. A famous phrase sums him up as 'The wisest fool in Christendom'.

He enjoyed writing and arguing. He published collections of verse as well as books on the paranormal, political theory, and the health-hazards of smoking. He personally supervised the team of scholars and bishops who produced the Authorised Version of the Bible in 1611, one of the greatest glories of the English language. It was dedicated to James as 'principal mover and author of the work'.

He it was who thought up the term 'Great Britain', which he introduced to recognise the fact that England, Wales and Scotland had at last become united, after a fashion, under his kingship.

He also introduced two sports into England: 'horse-running' and the Scottish game of golf.

The early years of James's reign coincided with the greatest period of Shakespeare's writing. James himself supported Shakespeare's company with the title of 'The King's Players', and in compliment to the new king and his interest in witchcraft, Shakespeare produced his Scottish tragedy, *Macbeth*. Ben Jonson and Inigo Jones also wrote court entertainments for him.

However, on the whole James was a weak and foolish king. Discontent grew more and more as he insisted on his 'Divine Right' to rule without any need to take advice from Parliament. His eccentric ways and homosexuality did nothing to make him popular.

CHARLES I

Reigned 1625-1649

Born 19.11.1600 in Dunfermline Palace, Scotland

Beheaded 30.1.1649 in Whitehall, London

Son of James I and Anne of Denmark

Married Henrietta Maria of France

Four sons and five daughters

His life unfolds like some remorseless Greek tragedy. Even now, wreaths appear round his Whitehall statue on the anniversary of the day when he was solemnly beheaded.

He succeeded to the throne when he was 24, and his deeply-held conviction that he ruled by 'Divine Right' coloured everything he did. He believed quite literally that he had God's authority to do whatever he wished. Three times he dissolved Parliament, and for eleven whole years he tried to rule the country by himself.

He relied for advice on his friend the Duke of Buckingham. Then, when Buckingham was stabbed to death in Portsmouth, Charles turned more and more to his wife Henrietta Maria and to Tom Wentworth, whom he created Earl of Strafford.

Parliament found an excuse to execute Strafford for treason and then publicly rebuked Charles for his poor kingship, in its famous 'Grand Remonstrance'.

The whole situation boiled over into Civil War in 1642. Battles, skirmishes, sieges, imprisonments, foiled attempts to escape: the next few years are a confused tale of kingly incompetence and parliamentary determination. Oliver Cromwell, M.P. for Huntingdon, increasingly found himself taking over the country.

Eventually it seemed that the only way of getting rid of an embarrassment was to send Charles to the execution block. It was a kind of ritual sacrifice, in which the victory of Parliamentary government over the arbitrary will of a monarch demanded the public death of a victim.

The hapless Charles walked with superb dignity from the Banqueting House in Whitehall to the scaffold in the road outside and spoke with courage to the crowds which had assembled to watch his execution.

"I go from a corruptible to an incorruptible crown, where no disturbances can be," he declared.

He was buried, rather surreptitiously, in St George's Chapel, Windsor.

OLIVER CROMWELL

'Lord Protector' 1653-1658

Born 1599 in Huntingdon

Died 1658 in Westminster

Strictly speaking, Oliver Cromwell should not appear in these pages, as he was never king. All the same, he was offered the crown, and had all the power and dignity of a king during the brief period when he was 'Lord Protector'.

He was born at Huntingdon, son of Sir Henry Cromwell of Hinchinbrook, and became MP for Huntingdon. He quickly became well-known for his passionate speeches against the king.

During the Civil War Cromwell showed outstanding military capacity and after Charles had been beheaded he became Chairman of the Council of State.

In December 1653 he was declared 'Lord Protector' and thus virtually became a dictator, ruling by decree. "You would scarcely notice any change," wrote the French Ambassador to his Government, "except that in the place of the King, the throne is occupied by Mr Cromwell, arrayed in purple velvet edged and lined with ermine."

Dictator though he was, Oliver Cromwell did his best to reconcile opposing factions: he is known to have deplored the persecution of Catholics, and he allowed Jews back into England, banished since the time of Edward I, four centuries before. However, like any dictator, Cromwell did not tolerate any opposition, and he has never been forgotten or forgiven by the Irish for his ruthless massacres at Wexford and Drogheda during the Civil War.

He did not live long as Protector, and passed the title to his third son, Richard. But Richard did not have his father's strength of character, and lasted in office for only a few months. People were longing for the monarchy to be restored.

RICHARD CROMWELL

Born 1626; Died 12.7.1712 in Hursley, Hants.
"Lord Protector II" September 1658-May 1659.
Third son of Oliver and Elizabeth Cromwell.

One has to be sorry for 'Idle Dick', the son of Oliver Cromwell. When his father died he was given a magnificent installation ceremony in Westminster Hall, becoming Lord Protector II. But he simply could not cope with the job he inherited.

After the Restoration, Richard fled abroad, living under the assumed name of 'John Clarke'. He returned to England in 1680, lived to a ripe old age, and is buried in the village church at Hursley, in Hampshire.

THE CIVIL WAR 1642-6 and 1648-51

The Civil War was a turning-point in English history. After King Charles I was defied, defeated and executed, the monarchy was never the same again.

Charles lacked the qualities of leadership, and was out of touch with the common people. He ignored parliament, raised unpopular taxes, and seemed to be bringing back the Catholic faith. When he tried unsuccessfully to arrest five rebellious MPs in their own House of Commons, it seemed inevitable that full-scale civil war would result.

The first act of defiance was at Hull in April 1642, when Charles was refused access to an arsenal for use against the Parliamentarians. A few weeks later, on 22 August, Charles raised his own standard in Nottingham. All told, there were about 600 battles, skirmishes and sieges, and there are many places throughout the country which bear witness to the bitter struggles between Parliamentarian 'Roundheads' and the Royalist 'Cavaliers'.

The main battles in the First Civil War (1642-6) were: Edgehill (Warwickshire), 23 Oct. 1642; Newbury (Berkshire), 20 Sept 1643 and again 27 Oct 1644; Marston Moor (near York), 2 July 1644; and Naseby (Northants), 14 June 1645. Fighting continued until May 1646, when Charles gave himself up. He was put on trial and executed on 30 January, 1649.

Meanwhile, Royalist forces tried to stage a comeback, helped by the Scots. However, they were again defeated at Preston (Lancs), 20 Aug. 1648; Dunbar (Lothian), 4 Sept 1650; and the final and decisive battle at Worcester, 3 Sept 1651. After this battle, Charles's son, the future Charles II, had to hide in an oak tree to escape capture (giving us countless pubs named 'The Royal Oak' to commemorate the event), but made his way to France, where he lived in exile until Cromwell's death and the collapse of the Commonwealth.

Cromwell's part in the Civil War started when he raised a troop of cavalry, which he led in the Battle of Edgehill. He formed and trained his formidable band of 'Ironsides'; his cavalry charge won the day at Marston Moor; and under the supreme command of Thomas Fairfax he led the victory at Naseby.

Cromwell's further battles in the Second Civil War (1648-51) included his victories at Preston, Dunbar and Worcester, and he stamped out opposition in Ireland by massacring garrisons at Drogheda and Wexford.

As architect of victory, he became Chairman of the Council of State after Charles's execution, and in December 1653 he was proclaimed Lord Protector.

CHARLES II

Reigned 1660-1685

Born 29.5.1630 in St. James's Palace

Died 6.2.1685 in Whitehall Palace, London

Son of Charles I and Henrietta Maria

Married Catherine of Braganza

No legitimate children, but 13 known illegitimate ones

Charles had an eventful childhood, being involved in many of the battles of the Civil War, but as the royalist situation worsened his father told him to join his mother Henrietta Maria in Paris. He was only 19 when he heard of his father's execution, and burst into tears as the messengers bringing the bad news called him "Your Majesty". Naturally he wanted to claim his kingdom. But how? That was the question which he had to face for the next eleven years.

His first idea was to try to gain a foothold in Scotland, for he was King of Scotland as well as King of England. Accordingly, he landed in Scotland, where he was crowned king in the parish church of Scone on 1 January, 1651. Then, as soon as he could, later that year, he crossed the border, marching south. Cromwell marched north to meet him and the two armies met at Worcester.

The Battle of Worcester took place on 3rd September, 1651, and from the top of Worcester Cathedral Charles sadly watched the defeat of his Scottish army. The next six weeks were exciting as he travelled, often in disguise, to the south coast to escape again to France.

For the next nine years Charles was a king in waiting; often poor, frequently in humiliating circumstances. It was a strange but useful apprenticeship, but at the end of this exile there was an almost tangible yearning in England to bring back the monarchy, and Charles was received with rapture when he rode into London on his thirtieth birthday to claim his birthright.

He was to become an extraordinarily popular monarch. He was head and shoulders more cultured and cosmopolitan than his predecessors. His exile in France had given him sophisticated tastes. Theatres were re-opened in England; classical standards began to be established in all the arts; and almost immediately on his return Charles set his personal seal of approval to the prestigious scientific body, the Royal Society.

Charles's own attitude, mocking, good-humoured, relaxed and self-indulgent, seemed to rub off on to his age. The ferocious bigotry of the Puritans was brought to an end. Good manners, rather than sectarian debate, were now seen to be important.

Much has been written about Charles's mistresses. He had many. And he had many bastards: he was kind to all thirteen of them, eight sons and five daughters, giving them honour and titles. To this day the aristocracy of England is peopled with descendants of Charles II. But the nation took his foibles to its heart, and even today the mention of Nell Gwynne – just one of his many mistresses – suggests a happy sense of jollity and good fun.

In fact Charles did bring a sense of fun to the monarchy. He had an intuitive understanding of the ordinary people. He said to his brother James, who was a totally different kind of human being: “don't worry, Jamie, they'll never kill me to make you king!”

However, James was his inevitable heir, for despite the thirteen bastards, no legitimate heir was forthcoming. So James, his brother, succeeded to the throne when Charles very suddenly and unexpectedly died in 1685.

CHARLES AND HIS MISTRESSES

A full list of mistresses would be impossible: his first love was Lucy Walter, who died before he became king: it was their son who was to become the Duke of Monmouth, and who tried to claim the throne when his father died.

The other main concubines were: Barbara Palmer (later to become Lady Castlemaine and the Duchess of Cleveland); Frances Stuart (known as 'la Belle Stuart, and who perhaps actually held Charles at bay); Hortense Mancini, Duchess of Mazarin; Louise de Kerouälle (who had been sent to England as a spy by Louis XIV); and of course Nell Gwynne, a lively comic actress at Drury Lane Theatre.

Perhaps without realising it we see a picture of Frances Stuart every time we look at a figure of Britannia on our coins, for she was the original model for this.

Once, someone asked Charles just how many women he'd had. Charles thought for a moment and then said thirty-nine. He explained that the number of Articles of the Anglican Faith was the right total for the Head of the Church of England.

Charles's wife, Catherine of Braganza, had to suffer much humiliation, and on his deathbed Charles begged her forgiveness. They had had no children.

JAMES II

Reigned 1685-1688

Born 14.10.1633 in St. James's Palace

Died 6.9.1701 in St. Germain-en-Laye, France

Son of Charles I and Henrietta Maria

Married (i) Anne Hyde

(ii) Mary of Modena

Four sons and four daughters by Anne Hyde
and two sons and five daughters by Mary of Modena

James reigned almost four years, and in that time his sheer incompetence led to a unique revolution – the 'Glorious Revolution' of 1688 – after which the very nature of monarchy in England underwent a profound and lasting change. Indirectly, then, we must be grateful to him for this.

His first crisis on reaching the throne was the rebellion of his bastard nephew, the Duke of Monmouth. He was able to quell this, but the terrible punishments meted out by Judge Jeffreys on those who supported the rebellion did nothing to help the popularity of James.

His unpopularity increased as he systematically filled every post possible with Catholics: judges, army commanders, academics. It was clear that James was attempting the reconversion of England.

Matters came to a head when his second wife had a sudden and rather premature baby – a boy. There were rumours that this was a plot, and that the queen had not been pregnant at all, but that the boy had been smuggled into St James's Palace in a warming-pan. Clearly the child was destined to be the next Catholic king of England!

The popular outcry was that this simply must not happen, and James's Protestant opponents invited William of Orange to come to England, with force if need be, to take the kingdom and become its Protestant King.

James's position became untenable as his supporters drained away from him. He fled the country, dropping the Great Seal of England into the Thames as he did so.

THE 'JACOBITES'

'Jacobus' is the Latin word for 'James', so when King James II was forced to leave England at the time of the 'Glorious Revolution' in 1688, those who still supported him, even in exile, came to be known as 'Jacobites'.

At first, James II tried to regain the throne by invading Ireland, but he was defeated by William III at the Battle of the Boyne, 1690. Returning to France, he lived at St. Germain, just outside Paris. The French King Louis XIV gave him a pension to help him to survive. He died in 1701, aged 57.

'JAMES III' 'Reigned 1701 - 1766

'James III', also known as the 'Old Pretender', was the son of James II. He was the baby who was supposed to have been smuggled into St. James's Palace in a warming-pan, and who had been disguised as a bundle of washing when his mother, Mary of Modena, escaped to France.

He tried, rather half-heartedly, to land in Scotland and stage a Stuart come-back, but after a brief unsuccessful rebellion at Sheriffmuir, he was forced to flee back to the continent. France refused to receive him so he went to Rome, married, and had two sons, Charles and Henry.

'James III' is buried in St. Peter's, Rome.

'CHARLES III' 'Reigned' 1766 - 1788

'Charles III', otherwise known as the 'Young Pretender' or 'Bonnie Prince Charlie', was born in Rome, son of 'James III', the Old Pretender.

He too tried to claim the throne, landing in Scotland in 1745, aged 25, and won a military victory over George II's troops at Prestonpans. He then marched south to Derby, but then decided to return to Scotland, where his army was utterly routed at the Battle of Culloden, 1746.

This saw the end of Jacobite hopes. Charles returned to Rome, where he died in 1788. He too is buried in St. Peter's.

'HENRY IX', 'Reigned' 1788 - 1807

On the death of Bonnie Prince Charlie the Jacobite line was continued, at least in theory, by his brother Henry. He did not marry, as he had become a Cardinal in 1747, so with Henry's death the direct Stuart line died out.

WILLIAM III and MARY II

William III reigned 1689-1702

Mary II reigned 1689-1694

William born 4.11.1650 in The Hague, Holland

Died 8.3.1702 in Kensington Palace

Mary born 30.4.1662 in St. James's Palace

Died 28.12.1694 in Kensington Palace

Daughter of James II and Anne Hyde

No children

William and Mary were cousins, sharing Charles I and Henrietta Maria as their common grandparents. William was the son of James II's sister Mary, who had married the Stadtholder of the Dutch Republic: Mary was the daughter of James by his first wife, Anne Hyde, who had died when James was still Duke of York and Mary was just nine.

The marriage was a genuine success, and as they were both Protestants, it seemed to the English parliament that they would make suitable replacements for James II, when it was clear that he was desperately unpopular and losing control, particularly because of his religious policies.

The essential point to remember in the succession of William and Mary is that they were brought to become monarchs at the behest of Parliament. No longer were kings and queens regarded as somehow the instruments of God.''Divine Right' was buried for ever, and the 'Glorious Revolution' of 1688 began an entirely new phase in the history of British Monarchy. From then on, it has remained a 'Constitutional Monarchy', in which the Sovereign owes his or her position to the will of the people.

Strictly speaking, it was Mary who was in line to the throne, but William refused to be subjugated to the role of a mere consort. As for Mary, she was completely dominated by William, and insisted that he should share the throne. Thus a curious situation arose, by which the monarchy was shared between them.

In practice it was William who made all the decisions but Mary remained in control whenever William was abroad.

Sadly, Mary did not live long to enjoy her reign. Smallpox killed her, aged only 32 and childless. Purcell composed magnificent music for her funeral in Westminster Abbey.

As for William, he was never popular. He had a silent, off-handed manner and was considered to be boorish and vulgar. Nevertheless he was an able man, a brave and capable military commander and despite his silence, a master of languages.

Perhaps the most permanent memorial of his reign today is Kensington Palace, for it was William who bought 'Nottingham House' there, having it rebuilt by Christopher Wren, and turning it into a new royal palace. It was during his reign that the old Whitehall Palace was completely destroyed by fire.

William fought resistance in Scotland and Ireland and struggled with Louis XIV in the Nine Years War. Supporters of the exiled James II were always a source of worry to him.

He died as a result of a riding accident, when his horse stumbled over a mole-hill. No monument marks the place where he is buried. He was put in the vaults of Westminster Abbey.

THE 'LITTLE GENTLEMAN IN BLACK VELVET'

Few people mourned the death of King William, and those who wished to see the return of the Old Pretender would frequently raise their glasses to the "little gentleman in black velvet" – (i.e. the mole who had provided the convenient stumbling-place for William's horse).

Another secret formula used by Jacobite sympathisers was to drink a toast "to the King over the water" and if they wished to conceal their allegiance they would merely hold their drinking-glasses over finger-bowls on the dining-table, thus toasting the King "over water".

Needless to say, when this secret sign was discovered by the Hanoverian monarchs, finger-bowls were banished from English royal tables. It was not until early in the twentieth century that Edward VII felt it safe enough to re-introduce finger-bowls for his guests.

ANNE

Reigned 1702-1714

Born 6.2.1665 in St. James's Palace

Died 1.8.1714 in Kensington Palace

Daughter of James II (before he became king) and Anne Hyde

Sister of Mary II

Married Prince George of Denmark

No surviving children, but she bore 17, including miscarriages

All her contemporaries speak of her dullness. She had no conversation, except gossip and took very little intelligent interest in the brilliant achievements of the writers, artists, architects and thinkers who were creating an age of elegance around her. It is almost ironic that the description 'Queen Anne' when referring to objets d'art, signifies exquisite taste and classical beauty.

Great battles were fought and won in her name by the Duke of Marlborough: Blenheim, Ramillies, Oudenarde, Malplaquet. The Treaty of Utrecht in 1713 gave England great power and influence. And in 1707 England and Scotland were at last formally united in the Act of Union.

But as for the woman herself, Anne was hardly ever more than an object of mild ridicule. She suffered terribly from gout, becoming increasingly so fat and heavy that she could hardly move, and had to be carried, pushed and wheeled about, even having to be lowered through trapdoors. Only one of her 17 children survived more than a few months: William Henry, Duke of Gloucester, but he died aged 11.

It is easy to poke fun at poor Queen Anne, but we owe her thanks for the development of Kensington Palace and the gardens and Orangery designed by Wren. Furthermore, she was noted for her generosity. 'As to her privy purse,' wrote one of her courtiers, 'it was a perpetual fund of charity.'

She died aged fifty and was buried in Westminster Abbey, the last of the Stuarts.

Although it is recorded that on her deathbed Anne expressed a wish that her nephew 'Bonnie Prince Charlie' should succeed her, there was a general reluctance to bring back a Catholic monarch, and so a different line of kings now had to be imported.

GEORGE I

Reigned 1714-1727

Born 28.5.1660 in Osnabrück, Germany

Died 11.6.1727 in Osnabrück, Germany

Son of Ernest Augustus, 1st Elector of Hanover and Princess Sophia

Married Sophia Dorothea of Celle

One son and one daughter

On the death of Queen Anne there was no nearer Protestant claimant to the English throne than George, whose mother was a granddaughter of King James I. Accordingly he was invited to become the next King of England.

He could not speak English, and so had to struggle with French or Latin to communicate with anyone not knowing German. It is not surprising that during his twelve-year reign he actually spent more time back in Hanover than in England.

He was unpopular not just because of his boorish manners and preposterous mistresses, but also because of the fact that he kept his wife in perpetual imprisonment in Ahlden Castle in Germany, on suspicion of adultery. Nevertheless, despite his unpopularity, people still preferred the thought of a German protestant to that of a Catholic Jacobite.

Two good things resulted from his reign: the growing strength of the 'Prime Minister' – Robert Walpole – thus effecting a swing to the power of Parliament; and the fact that Handel settled in England, thus giving an immense impetus to British music.

George I suffered a stroke while visiting Osnabrück and died in the very same room in which he had been born, sixty-seven years before.

A RIVAL KING

Throughout the entire reigns of George I and George II, the 'rival king' – the Stuart 'Old Pretender' – was actually still alive. 'James III' *(see page 59)* enjoyed a 'reign' of over sixty-four years, from 1701 (on the death of his father, the exiled James II), to his own death in 1766 – well into the reign of King George III.

If it had been a genuine reign it would have been the longest in English history.

GEORGE II

Reigned 1727-1760

Born 30.10.1683 in the Herrenhausen Palace, Hanover

Died 25.10.1760 in Westminster

Son of George I (before he became king) and Dorothea of Celle

Married Caroline of Ansbach

Three sons and five daughters

His was a long reign, over thirty-three years, and during that time, thanks to his able ministers and military commanders, the strength and influence of Great Britain grew apace.

George threw himself into battle. At the relatively advanced age of sixty-one he led an army of British, Germans, Austrians and Dutch to a conclusive victory over the French at the Battle of Dettingen. For a while George actually achieved popularity. This was the last occasion when an English reigning monarch fought in battle.

In 1759, the year before he died, England's military expansion led to conquests in Canada, India, and the Caribbean, and we achieved complete mastery of the seas. In many respects it was a successful reign. But it was largely due to other men. Power was draining from the monarch; the real wielders of influence were Walpole and Pitt.

George was the last king to be buried in Westminster Abbey. His son Frederick had died a few years previously, so the throne passed to his 22-year-old grandson, another George.

'POOR FRED'

England should have had a King Frederick. King George's eldest son, Frederick Louis, was expected to succeed the throne. Born in 1707, he enjoyed popularity; however, like many heirs to the throne, he died prematurely.

He was a keen player of the newly-invented game of cricket, and in the summer of 1748 he was hit hard on the chest by a cricket-ball while playing at his summer residence, Cliveden House, in Buckinghamshire. An abscess resulted and was the cause of his early death in 1751.

George II hated him, writing; "I have lost my eldest son, but was glad of it."

GEORGE III

Reigned 1760-1820

Born 4.6.1738 in Norfolk House, St. James's Square, London

Died 29.1.1820 in Windsor Castle

Son of Frederick, Prince of Wales and Augusta of Saxe-Coburg-Gotha

Married Charlotte of Mecklenburg-Strelitz

Nine sons and six daughters

George reigned for almost sixty momentous years. The British Empire was strengthened; America was lost; Australia was discovered; France erupted and guillotined its king. Meanwhile, life was being transformed by the Industrial Revolution.

Throughout this time, George patronised the arts and sciences. He entertained the boy Mozart and his father when they came to London. His books formed the foundation of the British Museum Library. He also busied himself in agricultural schemes and model farms, so that he gained the nickname of 'Farmer George'.

In his prime he was a successful and popular king, and a more than successful father, inasmuch as his wife Charlotte produced baby after baby virtually annually, until they had a family of fifteen. 'My quiver is full', he remarked, after the last had been born.

It was his personal tragedy that he finally became so mentally sick that he had to be restrained in a straight-jacket and kept as a pathetic prisoner in a padded chamber in Windsor Castle. In his final years his long white beard and rambling words gave him the appearance of a crazed King Lear.

He lived over ten years in seclusion and outlived poor Charlotte. But people remembered him with affection.

KING OF MANY LANDS

King George III was the last King of America: the thirteen American colonies recognised his authority until 1776. He was also King of most of the West Indies; Canada; Sierra Leone, from 1787; Gambia, 1716; New South Wales, from 1788; parts of India; Ceylon (now Sri Lanka) from 1795; Singapore, from 1819; Cape Colony, from 1806; Gibraltar; Malta, from 1800; Ionian Islands, from 1814; and King of Hanover. This is not a full list, but serves to show how British influence was growing during his reign.

GEORGE IV

Reigned 1820-1830

Born 12.8.1762 in St. James's Palace

Died 26.6.1830 in Windsor Castle

Son of George III and Charlotte of Mecklenburg-Strelitz

Married (i) Mrs. Maria Fitzherbert (in secret)

(ii) Caroline of Brunswick

One daughter, by Caroline

George reigned for nine years as Regent before becoming king, so the word 'Regency' applies to the period 1811-1820, when he was standing in for his mad father.

From his early teens he was sexually voracious and enjoyed a huge number of mistresses, but the only woman for whom he apparently had a lasting love was a Catholic widow, Mrs. Fitzherbert. He actually married her, secretly, but had to have the marriage annulled in order to marry an official wife, virtually chosen for him by parliament, Caroline of Brunswick, whom he detested at first sight.

George IV's sex life and drinking orgies were the scandal of his time, and he appeared to have no remorse or inhibition. His treatment of his wife was publicly callous, and at his coronation he gave orders for her to be refused entry to Westminster Abbey. She tried to get in, but had to go away, humiliated.

But despite his appalling behaviour and extravagance, his other claim to fame was as a patron of the arts. He was a genuine connoisseur of painting, architecture, literature and all the arts. Brighton Pavilion is a monument to his eccentric and flamboyant taste, but this was merely an escapist holiday retreat.

His main gifts to posterity were his improvements to London. We owe a debt of gratitude to George and his architect John Nash not only for the strange Brighton Pavilion but also for the elegant Regent's Park and the magnificent Regent Street in London.

But by far his most important legacy is Buckingham Palace. Against all argument and objections he pushed forward his scheme for enlarging Buckingham House into a new palace. In hindsight we must be grateful to him. London simply would not have been as it is today without him.

It has to be said, however, that George had very little to do with the great events of his time.

Charlotte, his only child, had died in childbirth, so the throne passed to George's younger brother, William.

WILLIAM IV

Reigned 1830-1837

Born 21.8.1765 in Buckingham Palace

Died 20.6.1837 in Windsor Castle

Son of George III and Charlotte of Mecklenburg-Strelitz

Married Adelaide of Saxe-Meiningen

No legitimate children

William's reign was brief, just under seven years. But it was an explosive and momentous time. Much against William's will the great Reform Bill was passed in 1832. It is impossible to overstate the importance of this. For the first time voting rights were given to the middle classes. It was a constitutional change of immense significance. In later years further Acts were to be passed, giving the vote to other classes, but the Reform Bill, in William's reign, marked the first of these great changes.

Clearly a major result of this change was that the monarchy lost political power. William desperately tried to stem the tide of democracy, and at one time abruptly dismissed parliament in order to try to change the party in power. However, he had to admit political defeat. Since his day, the sovereign has had to adjust increasingly to a neutral role, being 'above politics'.

In himself, William was a colourful character. He had genuinely enjoyed his life at sea, and had joined his first ship as a midshipman aged just 13. He had no privileges, and ate, drank, swore, gambled, whored, just like any rough-and-tumble teenager in the navy.

He actually visited New York while the British flag was still over it, the first and only English monarch – albeit a future monarch – to see America as a colony. His life at sea included taking part in a naval battle, and he became a close friend of Nelson.

He hated airs and graces, and in his way he was liked for his bluff, good natured, rather eccentric outspokenness. After the scandals of his brother, George IV, he restored respect for the monarchy.

As he did not produce a legitimate heir, the throne passed to his niece, Victoria.

VICTORIA

Reigned 1837-1901

Born 24.5.1819 in Kensington Palace

Died 22.1.1901 in Osborne House, Isle of Wight

Daughter of Edward, 1st Duke of Kent and Victoria of Saxe-Coburg

Married Prince Albert of Saxe-Coburg-Gotha

Four sons and five daughters

Victoria was the longest-reigning English monarch: 63 years and 216 days. She restored dignity and mystique to the throne and gave her name and character to a great age in Britain's development.

It is a pity that the common image of Queen Victoria is that of a dumpy, grumpy, glum-looking woman. The fact is that in many respects she was quite the opposite. As a young woman she was slim, beautiful, lively, and full of laughter. But because she lived for so long most of her subjects never remembered her in her prime.

Luckily, there is a vast amount of material about Victoria. Not only was she such a compelling and fascinating personality that everyone who met her simply had to record the experience, but also she herself was a prolific diary-writer and wrote a book about herself and her family. The result is that we know more about her than about almost any other monarch.

She came to the throne aged only 18. She married her cousin, Prince Albert, when they were both 20, and despite her intense dislike of child-bearing, they had nine children.

Then, after an idyllic marriage of 21 years, Albert suddenly died of typhus. Victoria was totally devastated. For the remainder of her reign – another forty years – she wore the heaviest of mourning, was hardly ever seen in public, and lived as a recluse on the Isle of Wight. Buckingham Palace remained dead and empty and her ministers had to travel to Osborne House to see her.

Meanwhile, the British Empire grew in power and strength; new parts of the world were explored; the industrial revolution transformed society; the modern world with its railways and telephones grew up around her.

Eventually, when she died in 1901, her children and grandchildren were so numerous, occupying virtually every throne in Europe and Russia, as a result of so many diplomatic marriages, that she became known as the 'Grandmother of Europe'.

Despite her reclusiveness – or perhaps even aided by it – she acquired an extraordinary mystique, particularly in her later years. She seemed to embody everything that was noble and precious about England and its Empire. Her two Jubilees, in 1887 and 1897, marking the fiftieth and sixtieth anniversaries of her coming to the throne, boosted her popularity to unprecedented heights. No previous English monarch ever came to be loved and revered so much as Queen Victoria.

The basic facts of her life are simply stated. But it is virtually impossible to convey in a short space the vivid intensity of her personality. She had unshakeable opinions on every issue, great or small, and was always totally convinced of the rightness of her views. In everything she was a person of extremes. Her love of Albert was ecstatic: her grief at his death was unremitting. She adored her Prime Minister Disraeli: she hated and humiliated Gladstone.

Her relations with her family were close, but fraught with tension, again because she always insisted on her own way. Unforgiveably, she never allowed her son the Prince of Wales and future King Edward VII to take the smallest part in running state affairs.

Although she did not consciously construct or innovate – apart, perhaps, from the Albert Hall and the Albert Memorial – nevertheless her name is found permanently embedded around the world: the Australian state of Victoria; the Victoria Falls in Zambia; Mount Victoria in Papua New Guinea: Victoria Island in the Canadian Arctic; capital cities, towns, parks, hospitals, railway stations, even sponge cakes. A full list would be impossible. The point is, she dominated her age.

More importantly, our whole conception of monarchy underwent a profound change during her long reign. She was not always popular; nevertheless because of her tenacious devotion to duty and her position as widow matriarch at the centre of a vast empire and network of royal relations abroad, she became a unique figure-head.

The concept of the 'royal family'; the idea of royal punctilious attention to detail and duty; the elevation of the monarchy to a beloved ideal: these were Victoria's intangible legacies. She transformed people's notions of what it meant to be 'royal'.

She was buried next to her beloved Albert in the tiny royal private chapel at Frogmore, in Windsor Park.

EDWARD VII

Reigned 1901-1910

Born 9.11.1841 in Buckingham Palace

Died 6.5.1910 in Buckingham Palace

Son of Queen Victoria and Prince Albert

Married Princess Alexandra of Denmark

Three sons and three daughters

Edward was clearly highly intelligent, a fine linguist, an excellent public speaker, and one who possessed an extraordinarily retentive memory.

His childhood, however, was complete disaster, as his father, Prince Albert, subjected him to an appalling regime of study and hard physical exercise, in an attempt to produce the perfect man. Edward quite naturally rebelled against this, and Queen Victoria was permanently displeased with him, never giving him any responsibilities, duties or training. He was fifty-nine when he succeeded to the throne.

On the face of it, the main part of Edward's life was simply round after round of pleasure: hunting, gambling, horse-racing, feasting. Frequently there were whiffs of scandal. Certainly he enjoyed many women, ate extravagantly and was once caught up in a law-suit about cheating at cards.

All the same, his love of travel was beneficial. As a 'freelance diplomatist' he helped enormously to further good relations between England and many other countries. After all, most of the kings and queens, dukes and princes were his own cousins and relations.

The result was that when he did eventually come to the throne, he was a natural go-between amongst the crowned heads of Europe. It was very largely due to him that the 'Entente Cordiale' between France and England was begun. Alas, despite strenuous efforts on his part, he never quite managed to get on with his cousin the German Kaiser, who always mistrusted him and thought he was trying to deceive him.

His reign was brief: not quite ten years. And when he died in 1910 the storm-clouds of a possible war with Germany were already gathering, much to his concern.

The nation sincerely mourned him as he was laid to rest in St George's Chapel, Windsor.

GEORGE V

Reigned 1910-1936

Born 3.6.1865 in Marlborough House, London

Died 20.1.1936 in Sandringham House, Norfolk

Son of Edward VII and Alexandra of Denmark

Married Princess Mary of Teck

Five sons and one daughter

With George V we come to a period well within living memory. To our present Queen Elizabeth II he was 'Grandpa England'. They adored each other and Archbishop Lang remembered seeing King George V on his hands and knees while the toddler Princess Elizabeth pulled him along by his beard. To him she was 'sweet little Lilibet'.

It was George's misfortune to live through the horrendous years of the First World War. It was a double tragedy for him, because of course many of his closest relations were German. Nevertheless, duty always came first, and he constantly visited the fighting areas to boost morale. He suffered a broken pelvis when thrown from his horse, but continued to meet people and decorate soldiers even from his sick-bed.

And when anti-German fever was at its worst, and even the royal family, with all its German connections, was suspected of anti-British activity, he made a dramatic gesture, changing the dynasty's name to that of Windsor, cutting off all remaining ties with Germany, and requiring other members of his family to change their German names for British ones (Battenbergs had to become Mountbattens, for example).

After the war things could never be the same. Modern transport, modern entertainments, modern means of communication, votes for women, socialism: a new world emerged. He did his best to adapt to the changing world and did his level best to act as a kind of referee in the post-war world, accepting the first Labour Government under Ramsay Macdonald with good grace, despite his inner misgivings.

The people of England came to love him for his transparent honesty and simplicity, and when he gave the first Christmas broadcast on radio in 1932, his popularity soared. His deep, comfortable voice sounded just as he looked: reliable, old-fashioned, reassuring.

He may have been a little naive, with his stamp collections and pet parrot, but he was certainly no fool. He must have seen the danger signals in the care-free unconventional behaviour of his son and heir, the future King Edward VIII and later Duke of Windsor.

"After I am gone," he confided to the Archbishop of Canterbury, "the boy will ruin himself in twelve months." It was a shrewd prophecy.

EDWARD VIII

Reigned from 20 January to 10 December 1936

Born 23.6.1894 in White Lodge, Richmond Park

Died 28.5.1972 in Paris

Son of George V and Mary of Teck

Married Mrs Wallis Simpson

The Abdication Crisis of 1936 seized the headlines momentarily, but today Edward VIII is no more than a foot-note in history.

Edward, as Prince of Wales, was dashingly modern, a part of the smart set of the twenties and thirties. He undertook many successful trips abroad and was wildly popular.

The trouble began when he met Wallis Simpson, an American divorcée. Edward seemed utterly mesmerised by her, showering her with expensive jewellery, and giving up other friends for her. The British public was kept completely in the dark until the story broke just about the time of George V's death.

In those days the whole affair seemed unthinkable. To marry a doubly divorced American was considered completely unacceptable. In any case, the unspoken thought was that at forty she was unlikely to bear children.

During his brief kingship Edward's ministers and courtiers were horrified by his casual approach to royal duties. Documents unread; appointments abandoned; tactless interference in foreign affairs. Visiting Germany with Wallis, he notoriously gave the Nazi salute when he met Hitler.

Stanley Baldwin, the Prime Minister, eventually gave Edward an ultimatum. It was to be either the throne or Wallis: he could not have both.

Edward abdicated in December 1936 and married Wallis the following June, quietly in France. He was given the title Duke of Windsor, but although Wallis became Duchess of Windsor, the title 'Her Royal Highness' was pointedly denied her.

During World War II the Duke became Governor of the Bahamas – it kept him out of the way. Then, after the war the couple lived in the outskirts of Paris. They travelled a little, played games, took 'holidays', entertained.

It was an an empty and useless life, and they knew it.

GEORGE VI

Reigned 1936-1952

Born 14.12.1895 in York Cottage, Sandringham

Died 6.2.1952 in Sandringham

Son of George V and Mary of Teck

Married Elizabeth Bowes-Lyon

Two daughters

When King Edward VIII abdicated, the line of succession was quite clear: the throne had to pass to his younger brother, Prince Albert, the Duke of York, known to his family as Bertie.

Bertie was horrified at the thought. He had never expected to become king. He had always been completely dominated by his elder brother and was quite content to be just a minor royal. He had an appalling stammer, which made it difficult for him to take on public engagements which involved speaking. Nevertheless, he had involved himself in all sorts of charitable activities, particularly among young people, and he was an excellent sportsman.

He had experienced the excitement of active service in the navy during World War I. Then after the war he married for love and had two daughters. The normality of his married happiness is, regrettably, almost unique in our kingly records.

Bertie took the title George VI, and despite his misgivings he became an exemplary king. His courage will never be forgotten as he and his Queen stayed in London throughout the blitz of World War II. Day after day the King and Queen moved among the people inspecting the latest night's destruction. They gave the country an example of unflinching loyalty to duty.

After the war George IV shared the austerity years with his people. He gave his assent to change after change as the post-war Labour Government set up the National Health Service, developed the welfare state, nationalised the major industries, and gave independence to India, thus stripping him of his title 'Emperor'. The British Empire itself ceased to exist, being replaced by a newer association of free states, the 'Commonwealth of Nations'.

As a constitutional monarch he had to agree to all these changes, but it meant that bit by bit, almost imperceptibly at first, and then increasingly swiftly, the very role and function of the monarchy was changing.

For fifteen years George performed the role of constitutional monarch with impeccable devotion. It is virtually impossible to find fault with the way he behaved, either in public or in private. He gained enormous respect for the way in which he carried out his duties, overcame his personal speech impediment, and handled every difficult situation with modesty and skill.

He died of lung cancer, and is buried in St George's Chapel, Windsor.

ELIZABETH II

Reigned 1952-

Born 21.4.1926 in 17 Bruton Street, London (now destroyed)

Daughter of George VI and Lady Elizabeth Bowes-Lyon

Married Prince Philip of Greece
three sons and one daughter

Queen Elizabeth II has been photographed, filmed, caricatured, adulated, gossiped about, possibly more than any other person. Yet, paradoxically, despite the crowds and intrusive press, she remains an extraordinarily private individual.

The facts are relatively simple. She was born in a private house in London with very little prospect of becoming a reigning monarch. Of course she had always moved in royal circles. Her grandmother, Queen Mary, took much care with her up-bringing, taking her to museums, concerts, exhibitions, and generally showing her what it was like to undertake royal duties. But it was her uncle's abdication that brought her suddenly and unexpectedly next in line to the throne.

She was thirteen when the Second World War broke out, and she lived throughout the London blitz in Buckingham Palace, sharing the bombs and rationing (her parents insisted on frugality) with her sister, Princess Margaret.

Towards the end of the war she begged to be allowed to do National Service "as other girls of my age do", and became Second Subaltern Elizabeth Windsor. It must have been a welcome taste of freedom and normality.

She fell in love with her distant cousin, Prince Philip of Greece: he was eighteen and she was thirteen when they first met. The wedding in 1947 provided the first bit of colour in drab, post-war Britain.

For a brief spell Elizabeth and Philip were able to enjoy a reasonably normal and private life together. Philip was keen to pursue his career in the navy, and as a serving officer's wife, Elizabeth lived for a while in Malta. However, her father's illness began to draw her more into the centre of things.

She and Philip were in Kenya when King George VI died. Quickly she returned, setting foot in England again as Queen Elizabeth II, aged 25, exactly the same age as Elizabeth I had been on her accession, four centuries before.

From South Africa in 1947 Elizabeth had made a noteworthy broadcast on the occasion of her twenty-first birthday. It took the form of an act of self dedication: "I declare before you all," she said, "that my whole life, whether it be long or short, shall be devoted to your service and the service of our great Imperial Commonwealth to which we all belong."

Several decades later we can see just how deeply she intended to keep that declaration. No sovereign has ever undertaken the monarch's role and duties with such tenacious integrity.

No age has seen more changes than the decades of her life. Rapid communications and easy transport have made it possible for her to travel more and be seen by more of her subjects than any of her predecessors. No monarch in history has travelled more than Queen Elizabeth II.

Probably the most far-reaching set of changes over which she has presided had been the dismantling of the British Empire. Country after country has acquired national independence, and yet the informal association of those countries into a new style of 'Commonwealth' has subtly given the role of the monarch an additional importance in holding these countries together.

But in all she does, it is crucial to remember that, as a 'constitutional monarch' she reigns, but does not rule. In other words, in practical terms she has no power. Nevertheless, by her presence, she prevents others from seizing it or misusing it.

The weekly meeting with the Prime Minister of the day is an important aspect of a sovereign's work. It is salutary that even the highest politician in the land has to feel accountable to someone even 'higher'. Not only does it keep a politician constantly on his toes, but also the fact that it is private and without political bias adds to the value of these weekly meetings.

Over the years she has amassed unrivalled experience. Winston Churchill and Harold Wilson are only two of her Prime Ministers who have felt embarrassment at the sharpness of her questioning."I shall certainly advise my successor to do his homework before his audience," said Harold Wilson, "or he will feel like an unprepared schoolboy."

Elizabeth II has made a magnificent and unique contribution to royal history. Despite crudely hostile newspaper headlines, the institution of the monarchy still has immense constitutional importance. Its role has become more subtle since the momentous Battle of Hastings. Who knows how it will evolve in the centuries to come?

KINGS OF SCOTLAND

The formation of the Kingdom of Scotland took place in 843 AD, when Kenneth MacAlpin (Kenneth I) King of Dalriada (the kingdom of the Scots) became King of Caledonia (the kingdom of the Picts).

Here is a list of Scottish kings from Kenneth I to James VI, who was invited to become the successor of Elizabeth I of England, reigning as James I of England. The dates given are the years in which they reigned. Some names have variant forms or spellings.

843-858	Kenneth I
858-862	Donald I (his brother)
862-877	Constantine I (son of Kenneth I)
877-878	Aedh (his brother)
878-889	Eochaid (nephew)
889-900	Donald II (Son of Constantine I)
900-942	Constantine II (son or descendant of Aedh)
942-954	Malcolm I (son of Donald II)
954-962	Indulf (son of Constantine II)
962-966	Dubh (Duff) (son of Malcolm I)
966-971	Culean (son of Indulf)
971-995	Kenneth II (son of Malcolm I)
995-997	Constantine III (son of Culean)
997-1005	Kenneth III (son of Dubh)
1005-1034	Malcolm II (son of Kenneth II)
1034-1040	Duncan I (his grandson)
1040-1057	Macbeth (married to Kenneth III's granddaughter Gruach)
1057-1058	Lulach (Macbeth's step-son)
1058-1093	Malcolm III (son of Duncan I)
1093-1094 and 1094-1097	Donald Bane (his brother) (deposed in 1094)

May-Nov 1094	Duncan II (son of Malcolm III)
1097-1107	Edgar (his half-brother)
1107-1124	Alexander I (his brother)
1124-1153	David I the Saint (his brother)
1153-1165	Malcolm IV (grandson of David I)
1165-1214	William I (The Lion) (his brother)
1214-1249	Alexander II (his son)
1249-1286	Alexander III (his son)
1286-1290	Margaret, 'Maid of Norway' (maternal granddaughter of Alexander III. Died aged 7 and never visited Scotland)
1290-1292	First interregnum.
1292-1296	John Balliol
1296-1306	Second interregnum.
1306-1329	Robert the Bruce
1329-1371	David II (his son) (reigning with interruptions)
1332 and 1333-1356	Edward Balliol (son of John)
1371-1390	Robert II (son of Walter the Steward and Marjorie Bruce, daughter of Robert I. Founder of the Stewart dynasty)
1390-1406	Robert III (his son)
1406-1437	James I (his son)
1437-1460	James II (his son)
1460-1488	James III (his son)
1488-1513	James IV (his son, who married Margaret Tudor, daughter of Henry VII of England)
1513-1542	James V (his son)
1542-1567	Mary, Queen of Scots (his daughter)
1567-1625	James VI of Scotland and I of England (son of Mary, Queen of Scots and Lord Darnley)

KINGS AND PRINCES OF WALES

After the Romans left, there were many local Celtic chieftains or kings, ruling various parts of Wales. Three main areas emerged: Gwynned, in North Wales; Powys, in north-central Wales; and Deheubarth, in South Wales.
By the middle of the 9th century the kings of Gwynned began to predominate. It is convenient to begin with 'Merfyn the Freckled', the King of Gwynedd who married Nest, daughter of the King of Powys.

825-844	Merfyn the Freckled
844-878	Rhodri I (Rhodri Mawr the Great) (his son)
878-916	Anarawd (his son)
916-942	Idwal the Bald (his son)
942-950	Hywel I (grandson of Rhodri I)
950-979	Iago I (son of Idwal the Bad)
979-985	Hywel II (Hywel the Bald) (his nephew)
985-986	Cadwallon (his brother)
986-999	Maredudd (grandson of Hywel I)
999-1005	Cynan (son of Hywel the Bad)
1005-1023	Llywelyn I (son-in-law of Maredudd)
1023-1039	Iago II (grandson of Iago I)
1039-1063	Gruffydd I (son of Llywelyn I)
1063-1075	Bleddyn ap Cynfyn (his brother)
1075-1081	rule by Arwystli
1081-1137	Gruffydd II (grandson of Iago II)
1137-1170	Owain (his son)
1170-1174	Cynan II (his son)
1170-1194	Dafydd (his brother) (ruled east Gwynedd)
1174-1195	Rhodri II (his brother) (ruled west Gwynedd)
1174-1200	Gruffydd III (son of Cynan II)
1194-1240	Llywelyn II (Llywelyn the Great) (grandson of Owain)
1240-1246	Dafydd II (his son)
1246-1282	Llywelyn III (Llywelyn the Last) (son of Gruffydd III) Llywelyn III entitled himself 'Prince of Wales' in 1258. He ruled the Principality; married Simon de Montfort's daughter; refused to pay homage to Edward I; was killed.
1282-1283	Dafydd III (his brother)

Edward I of England conquered the principality in 1283 and in 1301 gave the title 'Prince of Wales' to his son, later to become Edward II. Since that time there have been 20 first-born male heirs to the English throne who have been given the honorific title: 'Prince of Wales'.

IRISH KINGS

A full account of Irish Kings would be extraordinarily complex, and virtually impossible at this distance of time. In the early centuries of the Christian era Ireland was divided into about 150 small kingdoms.

Eventually these merged into five: Munster, Leinster, Meath, Connaught and Ulster. Dominance over the whole island under 'High Kings' came in 4th century, dating from the reign of Niall of the Nine Hostages, who reigned 379-405.

A series of 56 'High Kings' reigned from Niall until Ruaidri (1166-1186) and then Ireland came loosely under English domination.

The Irish Free State severed its links with the English monarchy at the abdication of Edward VIII in 1936 and became a republic, but Northern Ireland still retains the Queen as its Head of State.

THE ORDER OF SUCCESSION

At the time of publication (1996), after the death of Queen Elizabeth II, the order of succession is

1 – Prince Charles (born 14 November, 1948)

2 – Prince William (born 21 June, 1982)

3 – Prince Henry (born 15 September, 1984)

4 – Prince Andrew (born 19 February, 1960)

5 – Princess Beatrice (born 8 August, 1988)

6 – Princess Eugenie (born 23 March, 1990)

7 – Prince Edward (born 10 March 1964)

8 – Princess Anne (born 15 August, 1950)

9 – Peter Phillips (born 15 November, 1977)

10 – Zara Phillips (born 15 May 1981)

11 – Princess Margaret (born 21 August, 1930)

12 – Viscount Linley (born 3 November, 1961)

13 – Lady Sarah Chatto (born 1 May, 1964)

14 – Prince Richard, Duke of Gloucester (born 26 August, 1944)

QUEENS AND CONSORTS

Wives and mistresses of the early kings are barely mentioned. Sometimes a name may be recorded, but generally queens are very shadowy figures until after the Norman Conquest. However, this account of English Queens starts a little earlier, with Elfrida, widow of King Edgar. She enters our history books as a murderess. The deed took place on March 18th, 978 AD.

Elfrida (c960-c1020)

Second wife of King Edgar

Elfrida was a wicked step-mother. Her step-son was the young King Edward and her wickedness was that she murdered him. She wanted to put her own son Ethelred (the Unready) on the throne instead.

The event took place outside Corfe Castle in Dorset. King Edward, aged 15, was hunting in the area and decided to pay a visit to his step-mother and half-brother Ethelred who were living in the castle. The story goes that Queen Elfrida herself offered him a cup of wine as he was still sitting on his horse. On her command, just as he was drinking, one of her servants rushed forward and stabbed him. The horse galloped off, dragging the young king along on the ground, as his foot was still caught in the stirrup.

Edward himself became venerated as a saint and martyr, and Elfrida's conscience smote her so much that she founded a Benedictine Nunnery at Amesbury, near Stonehenge, where she retired to live a life of penance.

The Nunnery became a favourite residence of English queens and royal ladies, perhaps the most famous of whom was Eleanor of Provence, widow of Henry III (*see page 86*)

AMESBURY ABBEY

Nowadays many of the great and famous abbeys are in ruins or have completely disappeared following their destruction by Henry VIII. There is nothing left of Amesbury Abbey now, but in its days of importance it was linked with Fontevrault Abbey in France, where several English Kings and Queens are buried.

Ironically, one of Amesbury Abbey's last links with royalty, was a visit by Catherine of Aragon in 1501, on her way to marry Prince Arthur, elder brother of the future Henry VIII.

Emma of Normandy (Died1052)

Wife of the Saxon King Ethelred the Unready

Wife of the Danish King Canute

Emma is unique among English queens in that she was married to two kings (Ethelred the Unready and King Canute) and had sons by each of them who were also kings: Hardicanute (by Canute), and Edward the Confessor (by Ethelred).

She was reputed to have been extremely clever and beautiful when young, being called the 'Fair Maid'. In later years she became known as the wise 'Old Lady'.

It may have seemed a curious arrangement that Canute, who drove her first husband out of the country, should have taken her on as his wife, but it probably says much for her attractions that he was very keen to marry her. It was a happy and successful marriage.

There is an astonishing story about Emma in her second widowhood, in the reign of her son, Edward the Confessor. Apparently she was very friendly with Alwine, Bishop of Winchester, the city where she lived, and the friendship became something of a silly scandal. In order to prove her innocence, her son Edward ordered that she should undergo trial by ordeal.

Accordingly, she was required to step bare-footed over nine red-hot plough shares, heated and placed upon the floor of Winchester Cathedral. Led by two Bishops she stepped over them, and to everyone's great relief she was found to be completely unscathed. Her innocence was proved!

Her bones lie in a chest near the altar of Winchester cathedral. The chest also contains the bones of King Canute and the good bishop Alwine.

Queen Edith (Died1075)

Wife of Edward the Confessor

Edith was the daughter of the powerful Earl Godwin and sister of Edward's successor, King Harold. She had a reputation for charitable works but her life was somewhat curious as Edward is believed to have taken a vow of chastity. Unsurprisingly, they had no children.

On Edward's death she retired to Winchester, and it was left to her, after the Conquest, to hand over the city keys to William the Conqueror. It was a moment of high significance, as Winchester at that time was the capital of England. The Conqueror was kind to her and honoured her as a former Queen.

Queen Aldgyth

Wife of King Harold II

Harold's marriage to Aldgyth was openly a political one. She was the sister of Morcar and Edwin, Lords of Northumbria and Mercia, and Harold suggested marrying her in trying to reach a peaceful settlement with her brothers.

She was queen for only a few months, and fled, pregnant, to Chester when news of William's invasion reached London. Giving birth as a widow, she called her son Harold.

Edith of the Swan Neck

Mistress of King Harold II

Whether or not he was actually married to her, Edith was Harold's life-long partner and they had four sons and two daughters. It was left to Edith to help prepare Harold for battle at Hastings. Afterwards, the mangled corpses were so jumbled together that it was only Edith who could identify Harold, which she did by recognising the tattoo marks on his body.

Queen Matilda (Died 1083)

Wife of William the Conqueror

She was William's cousin,very petite, probably just over 4 feet tall. She was only about 16 when he proposed to her and he was about 20.

It was a considered a sin in those days to marry your cousin, but William defied the Pope, who had forbidden the marriage. They were both excommunicated, and pardoned only after each had promised to build an abbey. The two abbeys are still in existence today, in Caen, Normandy, and each of them is buried in the abbey they built.

She was enthusiastic about the project of invading England and personally gave William a specially-built flag-ship, beautifully decorated, for him to sail across the channel. William rewarded her by having her crowned as Queen in Winchester Cathedral.

William was a faithful husband, and when she died he was so grieved that he vowed he would give up his favourite sport, hunting. And he kept his promise.

It is impossible to know for certain whether Matilda had a hand in making the Bayeux Tapestry, but her name has been associated with it down the centuries.

Matilda of Scotland (1080-1118)

First wife of Henry I

Matilda's mother was descended from Alfred the Great and her father is well-known to students of English literature, for he was none other than the Malcolm who succeeded Macbeth as king of Scotland. He makes the final speech in Shakespeare's play.

During her teenage years Matilda was known as Edith, and was a none-too willing nun in Romsey Abbey, Hampshire, where her aunt was Abbess. Her aunt tried to force her to take the veil and become a nun, but Edith tore it off and stamped on it behind her aunt's back.

She made an excellent consort for Henry and was full of charity and good works. One of her main interests was encouraging road-building. One permanent memorial she left behind was the bridge at Stratford-le-Bow in London. It was the first arched bridge in England and was called a bow bridge. The bridge gave its name to the area.

Perhaps luckily for her she died before her husband and before the *White Ship* disaster in which her son William was drowned. But it was her daughter, also called Matilda, who became 'Lady of the English' in Stephen's reign, and whose son, Henry II, was the first of the Plantagenets.

Adela of Louvain (1103-1151)

Second wife of Henry I

After his heir had drowned, King Henry was desperate for another son, so he remarried, this time to a daughter of a French Count, Godfrey of Louvain. Adela (sometimes called Adelicia or Adelaide) was only 18; Henry was 54.

No son came; Henry died; and for a year Adela lived as a nun at Wilton, near Salisbury.

Then, as she was still young, she came out of mourning, married William de Albini, Duke of Norfolk, and seven of their children were to survive. Among the descendants of this marriage came two girls destined to become tragic queens: Anne Boleyn and Catherine Howard.

Adela spent her final years in a convent in Flanders.

Queen Matilda (c1103-1152)

Wife of King Stephen

There were so many Matildas at this time! This one was rather a shadowy figure. She gave Stephen her full support during the civil war, and helped to organise a rescue-bid when he was lying captive in Bristol castle.

She died two years before Stephen and was buried in Faversham Abbey, which she had helped to found.

Eleanor of Aquitaine (1122-1204)

Wife of Henry II

Everything about Eleanor was spectacular. Her long life was filled with every kind of excitement. A brief account cannot do her justice. There are many biographies of her: she compels attention.

She was brought up in the south of France, where poetry and the arts were so much more sophisticated than in the barbaric north. Aquitaine was a land of troubadours and courtly love, where marriage was merely incidental. Her tastes, her morals, her lifestyle: everything about her was different, and she brought a new dimension to the English court.

Two things stand out: she was sensationally beautiful and outstandingly rich.

Before she came to England she had been Queen of France, and when her husband King Louis went to the Holy Land on the Second Crusade she insisted on going too, and led a contingent of women to form a special 'ladies crusade'. In the Holy Land she had at least two amorous adventures.

When she met Henry Plantagenet, heir to the throne of England, she fell passionately in love with him, despite the fact that she was 12 years older. Quickly she divorced Louis, who put up no resistance, and six weeks later Henry and Eleanor were married. She was five months pregnant.

Two years later they were crowned, magnificently, in Westminster Abbey. Her silks and velvet, jewels and brocades, all from exotic lands, astonished everyone.

Henry's reign was an exhausting and turbulent one, in which she shared fully. She gave Henry five sons and three daughters, but eventually their marriage fell apart, especially as their sons grew up. She sided with them against their father, so Henry held her a virtual prisoner in Winchester for the last sixteen years of his life.

She was sixty-seven when Henry died and she could be released from prison. Yet her life was now just about to enter its most active period. Her son Richard the Lionheart was hardly ever in England, so she ruled in his name, passing popular laws, pardoning prisoners, and making sure things ran smoothly.

She organised a bride for Richard, Princess Berengaria of Navarre, and made the journey personally to Navarre, south of the Pyrenees, to negotiate the marriage arrangements. Then she took the bride-to-be to Sicily, leaving her to journey on to Richard, while she herself went back to England to sort out trouble with her too-ambitious youngest son, John.

When Richard was captured and held prisoner she organised the raising of the enormous sum required for his ransom. It cost everyone in England a quarter of a year's pay. But she managed to collect it, free Richard, and still retain popularity both for herself and for her son.

She survived her son King Richard, saw her other son John crowned as his successor, and then went back to Aquitaine to arrange another splendid marriage, this time with her granddaughter Blanche of Castile to the grandson of her former husband King Louis. She was energetic to the end.

Her tomb, in Fontevrault in France, next to her husband Henry II, has a magnificent effigy, a tribute to a great queen.

Berengaria of Navarre (1165-1230)

Wife of Richard the Lionheart

Berengaria never saw England. She was born in Navarre, married in Cyprus, and lived most of her life in France.

Her life was a strange and rather sad affair. Her reputation for beauty was wide-spread, and a marriage to Richard the Lionheart might well have seemed an ideal match.

But Richard was gay. He had no time for her. After marrying her in Cyprus he went on to his crusade, and left her to follow after. And when he lost the campaign he sent her to England by boat, saying that he would travel by land and meet up with her later.

But Berengaria never reached England. She probably never wanted to. There was a sort of reconciliation, and Richard promised to change his lifestyle, but by that time it was too late. Berengaria was with him when he died. She must have known that her life as queen had been a sham.

She was only about 34 when Richard died, but she never remarried. Instead, she retired to a nunnery and spent the rest of her life helping the poor, especially caring for abandoned children. She built a beautiful abbey in L'Epau, France, where she spent her life and where she was finally laid to rest.

Isabella of Angoulême (1186-1246)

Wife of King John

Isabella was only 14 when John married her in Bordeaux. They had five children but life with John must have been difficult. Once when he thought Isabella was having an affair he had the man hanged, and suspended the corpse above her bed.

The marriage lasted sixteen years and ended when John was poisoned. It must have been a great relief to Isabella.

Their son Henry was still only aged nine. It was a dangerous time, so rather than risk someone else claiming the throne Isabella acted promptly. They were in Gloucester at the time, a long way from London. She quickly proclaimed Henry king and had him crowned in Gloucester Cathedral. There was no crown to hand, so she simply used one of her golden collars.

She was still only thirty, so she was delighted to go back to Angoulême and marry the lover she had been forced to abandon when John had demanded her as his wife. It was a happy reunion and she bore her new husband three sons and several daughters.

Then came disaster. She was accused, probably wrongly, of conspiring to poison the king of France.

She fled to Fontrevrault Abbey, a place of sanctuary, and lived in hiding in a secret chamber there for the last two years of her life dying aged about sixty.

Many years later her son Henry III was upset to find that she had been buried in an open cemetery and ordered her remains to be moved inside the Abbey. She has a noble effigy there.

Eleanor of Provence (1222-1291

Wife of Henry III

Henry III was aged twenty-nine and had been king for twenty years when he married the fourteen-year-old Eleanor of Provence. He had made at least five unsuccessful attempts to find a wife, so he must have been pleased to welcome her.

Eleanor's arrival, marriage and coronation were marked with extravagance. London was transformed with costly and elaborate decorations. Unfortunately, everything else she did seemed equally wasteful and ostentatious. Thus she became one of our most unpopular queens.

People attributed much of their increased taxation to her extravagance, and it was widely believed her influence over the king was a result of witchcraft. It was felt that she was far too foreign, gave posts to her large retinue of followers from Provence, and refused to fit in with English ways.

Once, as she was going under London Bridge in her barge, the citizens above pelted her with rotten eggs and garbage, shouting 'Down with the witch! Let's drown her!'

She survived her husband Henry by almost 20 years and lived out the rest of her time quietly in a nunnery near Amesbury, close to Stonehenge *(See page 80).* It was the legendary resting-place of Queen Guinevere, wife of King Arthur.

She had learned her lesson about extravagance.

Eleanor of Castile (1244-1290)

First wife of Edward I

When Edward and Eleanor first met she was a ten-year-old Spanish princess and he was a tall teenager of fifteen, still heir to the throne. Edward's mother had been told by a fortune-teller that if the marriage was to prosper she and her son must arrive at Burgos, in Castile, where Eleanor's father was king, precisely on 5th August, 1254. This they did and the two royal youngsters were married on the spot.

When Eleanor arrived in England everyone was kind to her. King Henry III, her new father-in-law, made sure that her room in Guildford Castle had glass put into its windows and a special fire-place with a chimney was installed.

Their marriage was genuinely shared. They went together on a crusade, during which Eleanor saved Edward's life and nursed him back to health. On their way back to England they learned that King Henry III had died, so they were now King and Queen.

Edward's reign was filled with warfare for he was determined if possible to create a United Kingdom. He fought fiercely in Wales and when Eleanor gave birth to a son in Caernarvon Castle he made the baby, as a goodwill gesture, the first 'Prince of Wales'.

Edward was less successful in Scotland, and wrote to ask Eleanor to come up north to join him. But sadly she was taken ill on the way and died in the Lincolnshire village of Harby.

Eleanor of Castile – *continued*

Edward was desolate. He rushed back south, but could do nothing except make arrangements for her funeral. She had to be taken back to Westminster in stages, so he ordered a beautiful memorial cross to be erected in each of the stopping-places. In all there were twelve of these famous 'Eleanor Crosses' – the best known of all being the one built in the village nearest Westminster – Charing.

Nowadays 'Charing Cross' is a busy London railway station and in the forecourt is a tall monument – a Victorian replacement of the original Eleanor Cross, which used to stand at the top of Whitehall on the site now occupied by a statue of Charles I on horseback.

Edward ordered two wax candles to burn for ever by her tomb in Westminster Abbey. They burned for two and a half centuries, extinguished only at the time of the Reformation.

Margaret of France (1282-1317)

Second wife of Edward I

Much as he had loved Eleanor, Edward took a second bride, Margaret, a sixteen-year-old French princess. He was sixty by now; nevertheless they had three children.

Margaret was only 26 when Edward died and lived for only another ten years, during which time she busied herself helping the poor and encouraging the arts. In particular she helped to rebuild the church of the Greyfriars in London. She herself was buried there.

Isabella of France (1292-1358)

Wife of Edward II

Isabella's life is filled with unspeakable cruelties. Indeed her nickname was 'The She-Wolf of France'. Nevertheless she suffered cruelty as much as she inflicted it.

When she married Edward II her hopes must have been high. But when she realised that her new husband was openly and crazily in love with his gay partner Piers Gaveston she wrote home in misery to her father, King Philip the Bold of France.

She put a brave face on things and bore Edward two sons and two daughters, but after Gaveston was captured and beheaded by the barons who hated him Edward took up two new partners, the Despensers, father and son. It was then that she rebelled, took herself a lover, Roger Mortimer, recruited an army in France and waged war on her husband.

Edward was defeated, the Despensers were mutilated and killed. Hugh Despenser had his genitals cut off and had to watch his own bowels being burnt in front of him as he was hung up on a gibbet fifty feet high. Then Edward himself was murdered, with a red-hot poker being thrust up his anus.

Of course, her son Edward now became King. He was only 14, but obviously he had had enough of all this sordid business. The first thing he did was to arrest Mortimer and have him hanged. Then he put Isabella his mother under house arrest in a fortress at Castle Rising, Norfolk.

She stayed there for thirty-one years and went mad.

Philippa of Hainault (1314-1369)

Wife of Edward III

Hainault, where Philippa came from, is in Flanders. The Hainault in London has no connection with this at all. Like many Dutch or Flemish women Philippa was a hearty, buxom girl with lovely flaxen hair. No one ever spoke ill of her, and her influence was wholly good.

A well-known story gives some indication of her character. When she entered London as a bride in 1329 there was a great tournament held in her honour. A badly-made scaffold on which she and her ladies were sitting suddenly gave way and she fell alarmingly to the ground. Luckily, no one was hurt, but Edward III, her bridegroom, was absolutely furious and ordered the scaffolding contractor and his carpenter to be hanged.

Philippa fell to her knees and flatly refused to get up until Edward had changed his mind and pardoned them. "And so," wrote the historian Jean Froissart, who knew her well, "the people learnt to love her as no Queen was ever loved before or since."

At the time of this incident Philippa was only 14. It must have taken courage and determination to risk upsetting her new husband like that.

As she grew into a mature woman she brought wealth to England by encouraging the wool trade with her native Flanders, and acted as a well trusted regent when Edward was abroad.

They had twelve children, including the Black Prince, who was Prince of Wales and heir to the throne. Fortunately she did not live to learn of his death and could never have foreseen the power-struggle between the descendants of her other sons, the Lancastrians and Yorkists, during the years ahead.

She was only fifty-five when she died in Edward's arms.

Anne of Bohemia (1366-1394)

First wife of Richard II

Richard and Anne were both only 15 when they married, and the young couple seem to have been very fond of each other, sharing artistic tastes. She had a mania for extravagant clothes and introduced the horned head-dress into England. This absurd-looking affair stood two feet high: two cardboard horns decorated with gold and silver lace and blazing with jewels. As for Richard, he introduced shoes with long pointed toes, at least half a metre long.

This was the age of Chaucer. Pictures of the time show the astonishing and fantastic fashions which were being worn, largely as a result of Anne and Richard.

Anne also introduced the side-saddle for women. Again, it was a silly fashion, and running footmen were needed to help ladies keep their balance.

Anne was only 28 when she died of the plague, childless, in her palace at Sheen, in present-day Richmond.

She was given the most extravagant funeral yet seen in the country. A vast sum was spent on wax candles and torches. As for Sheen Palace, where she died, Richard simply could not bear to go there any more and ordered it to be demolished.

Isabella of Valois (1387-1410)

Second wife of Richard II

She must have been a bewildered little girl when she was told she must marry the King of England. After all, she was only aged eight.

Marry she must, so she left her father, Charles the Foolish of France, and went to live in Windsor Castle as Queen of England. Richard, her husband in name, visited her from time to time and made a fuss of her.

Then everything changed. Richard was deposed. A new king calling himself Henry IV was on the throne. And astonishingly, she was told to prepare for marriage with Henry's son, the future Henry V. They were then both aged 11.

She refused to have anything to do with the new régime, and eventually Henry let her go back to France where she belonged. She married again, but died in childbirth, aged 22.

MARY DE BOHUN

Never Queen, but first wife of Henry IV

History books do not often mention Mary de Bohun. After all, she died five years before Henry became king, so she never knew that royalty was in store for both him and her little son Henry, the future victor at Agincourt.

Her ancestor had come over with the Conqueror and had been made Earl of Hereford for his help. So, overthrowing kings was in her blood, too.

She bore Henry seven children in all, and was only 25 when she died, giving birth to their daughter Philippa in Leicester.

She was buried with great ceremony in the church of St. Mary de Castro in that city.

Joan of Navarre (1370-1437)

Second wife of Henry IV

Henry IV did not need to marry Joan. He had his heirs from a previous marriage. Nevertheless he felt it would be a good political move, so when Joan's husband, the Duke of Brittany, died, he invited her over to become his consort.

Joan originally came from Navarre, daughter of Charles the Bad, so she is known either as Joan of Navarre or Joan of Brittany.

There were no children, but they enjoyed ten happy years of marriage before Henry's sudden death. At first she got on well with her step-son, who succeeded to the throne as Henry V and for a while she was still treated with respect.

Then her step-son, the glorious victor of Agincourt, suddenly had her arrested, stripped of everything she possessed and forced her into prison. She was accused of being a witch!

She must have been terrified, for the penalty for witchcraft was being burnt alive. Joan of Arc was to die like this.

Evidence against her was flimsy but she languished in prison for three years until the last weeks of Henry V's life, and then his conscience prompted him to release her. She lived on in comfort well into the next reign and then was buried next to her husband in Canterbury Cathedral.

Catherine of Valois (1401-1437)

Wife of Henry V

Readers of Shakespeare know Catherine because of the memorable courtship scene in Shakespeare's play *Henry V*. She was part of the spoils of victory after Agincourt, and Henry and Catherine were married in Troyes just as the peace-treaty was signed. In fact she was the much younger sister of Isabella, who had married Richard II some years before.

They enjoyed a brief and happy marriage, but Henry died of dysentery only two years after, leaving Catherine a widow aged only 21, with a baby son of only nine months.

She took on the responsibility of bringing up the royal baby, Henry VI, and travelled many miles showing him off to the crowds. Then, in great secrecy, she took a lover and married him. His name, Owen Tudor. He was in fact just a common soldier who had been one of Henry V's bodyguards.

They had three children before the secret was out, and then the scandal broke. Catherine was banished to a nunnery and Owen Tudor clapped in Newgate Gaol. Later, Henry VI pardoned them both, acknowledged their children and made one of them Earl of Richmond. And it was his son Henry, the second Earl of Richmond, who became the first of the Tudor kings.

Catherine, then, became the grandmother of the Tudor dynasty.

She was buried in Westminster Abbey, where her body was rather gruesomely fondled and kissed by the diarist Samuel Pepys, almost two and a half centuries later. Queen Victoria had her remains properly laid at rest.

Margaret of Anjou (1430-1482)

Wife of Henry VI

Margaret was only 15 when she married Henry VI. At the time he was aged 22 and busily planning his new projects at Eton and King's College Cambridge. She herself was the first of the two queens who founded Queens' College, Cambridge, next door to King's. Everything looked promising for a happy marriage. However, she must have realised gradually just how weak-willed her husband was.

Henry lost his sanity completely for eighteen months and the ensuing power vacuum led to the Wars of the Roses. Hectic years followed and she began to take control, for Henry, even sane, was no soldier. Hers was a life of battles, defeats, victories, deaths and imprisonments. Henry had two periods of being king and then was quietly murdered in the Tower of London. Margaret, who had tried so hard to organise resistance, had the misery of seeing her son killed in the final battle at Tewkesbury, and then she herself was held captive in the Tower.

She had a reputation for cruelty and vindictiveness, but after all, she only tried to do her duty.

Eventually her aged father René paid out a vast ransom for her and she returned to France. She died aged 51 and is buried in Angers Cathedral.

Elizabeth Woodville (1437-1492)

Wife of Edward IV

According to tradition Elizabeth was a young and beautiful widow who asked the unmarried King Edward IV to help in restoring some land to her sons. They met by a tree later known as the Queen's Oak in the forest of Whittlebury.

By all accounts she was ravishingly attractive, with long blond hair: Edward was captivated. They were secretly married in the village church at Grafton in Northamptonshire.

The problem for Elizabeth was that she was a commoner – in fact she was the first non-royal queen since before the conquest. Edward's brother Richard disliked her intensely and considered her an upstart. As soon as Edward was dead he lost no time in putting her young uncrowned son, Edward V, in the Tower of London, declared her marriage to Edward IV illegal and her ten children bastards.

She fled to Westminster Abbey and lived there in sanctuary with all her young children around her. Their ages ranged from 17 to 3. Then her second son, Richard, was taken from her to join his elder brother in the Tower. There they were both murdered.

She was forced to go to another part of Westminster and for two years was humiliated by being known as 'Dame Gray, lately calling herself Queen of England'.

Richard's defeat at Bosworth came as a godsend. Her dignity was restored; her eldest daughter became Henry VII's bride; and she lived to see three sturdy grandchildren born – one of them to become Henry VIII.

Anne of Warwick (1456-1485)

Wife of Richard III

Like Elizabeth Woodville, Anne was English. She was the daughter of the Earl of Warwick ('Warwick the Kingmaker') and had been married to Richard as a part of her father's political manoeuvring.

When Richard became king she must have been somewhat surprised to find herself queen and her baby son declared to be Prince of Wales. However, Richard was determined to seal the process of acquiring royalty and gave Anne and himself a second coronation, in York, to make doubly sure.

But the reign was shortlived and Anne's part in it even shorter, for both she and her son died just before the Battle of Bosworth.

Elizabeth of York (1466-1503)

Wife of Henry VII

Despite the fact that it was a calculated move on Henry's part, to put a stop to the Wars of the Roses, the marriage was a happy one, fruitful and loving. No one ever accused either of them of being unfaithful.

After a wretched and terrifying childhood, Elizabeth's years as wife and queen were relatively tranquil. Four children arrived and Henry planned great futures for them all.

But sadly, her eldest, Prince Arthur, died aged 15, shortly after marrying Catherine of Aragon. Elizabeth was so grieved that it totally undermined her health. She lived for less than a year, and died aged 37, shortly after giving birth to another child.

She was given a superb funeral and her tomb in Westminster Abbey is one of the finest in the land.

But her universal memorial is in virtually every household, though few people are aware of it: for it is her portrait which we see as the Queen on every pack of cards.

Catherine of Aragon (1486-1536)

First wife of Henry VIII

She was destined to shape the course of English history in a profound manner, because of her inability to produce a son and heir for Henry VIII.

Originally she had been married to Arthur, Henry's older brother, but he had died of the plague, and Henry married the young widow just a fortnight before they were both crowned as King and Queen.

In the early years their marriage was a joy. Both were young, artistic and kept a brilliant court. London became a cultural centre as never before.

Henry was constantly surprising her with ingenious masques and unusual entertainments. Even the birth of a girl was a cause for merriment and rejoicing. "There will be other children," he said.

But the deaths and miscarriages went on and on. Henry persuaded himself that the marriage was cursed, and his neglect worsened into abuse.

Catherine's dignity, courage and refusal to bend to Henry's will in the matter of divorce will always earn her admiration. Her daughter Mary inherited much of this steely strength.

She died of cancer, aged 50 and was buried in Peterborough Cathedral.

Anne Boleyn (1507-1536)

Second wife of Henry VIII

It was widely believed that Anne Boleyn was a witch. She had so much influence over the king that only sorcery would explain it. Even Henry himself believed this. There were even physical oddities about her: a large mole on her neck, six fingers on her left hand.

By playing hard to get she inflamed Henry to a furious lust. The marriage was in secret and her daughter, the future Elizabeth I, was born eight months later.

Desperate for a son, Henry accused her of adultery and had her executed. Her remains were pushed into an old arrow-chest and buried at the Tower.

Jane Seymour (1506-1537)

Third wife of Henry VIII

The Spanish Ambassador described Jane 'as no great beauty, of middle stature: so fair one might almost call her pale.'

She was aged 33 when she gave birth to Edward. It was a difficult birth, but it was her moment of triumph. She had given the king what he had always wanted: a son and heir.

Alas, the excitement and fatigue were too much for her and within days she was dead. Of all Henry's wives, it is Jane who is buried next to him in St George's Chapel, Windsor.

Anne of Cleves (1515-1557)

Fourth wife of Henry VIII

Henry's adviser, Thomas Cromwell, decided that it would be useful to make a marriage link with Protestant Europe; Holbein produced a suitable portrait; the King approved; so Anne duly set sail for England.

Henry's disappointment was furious. He called her a 'Dutch cow' and a 'great Flanders mare'. Cromwell trembled for his life and was executed a few months later.

Nevertheless, Henry and Anne came to an amicable arrangement and Anne became Henry s official 'sister'. She lived in comfort and was buried in state in Westminster Abbey.

Catherine Howard (1522-1542)

Fifth wife of Henry VIII

She was 18 when she married Henry: he was 49. Once more, Henry married for love: the physical attraction was intense, while it lasted.

By all accounts her upbringing was astonishingly lax, and when Henry suspected her of adultery there were many stories about her riotous midnight escapades as a teenager. Henry seems to have gone quite mad with rage and jealousy. Catherine was not even allowed to speak in her own defence.

The heads of her supposed lovers were stuck on spikes over London Bridge. Catherine herself was beheaded on the same block of wood used six years before by Anne Boleyn. Her marriage had lasted 17 months. She was just 20.

Catherine Parr (1512-1548)

Sixth wife of Henry VIII

Catherine Parr had already been twice married before she became Henry's sixth wife. Both her previous husbands had been old men, but Catherine herself was still only thirty – young enough to provide a few more heirs.

Everyone spoke well of her; she seems to have been kind and sensible and told Henry it would be better to be his mistress rather than his wife.

By this time Henry was impossibly short-tempered and living in constant agony with his ulcerous leg. It was largely Catherine's skill as a nurse that saved her life, for she too was almost sent to the Tower for being too argumentative over religious matters.

She survived Henry; married again, to Thomas Seymour, brother of Jane Seymour, Henry's third wife; but died shortly after in childbirth.

Lord Guilford Dudley (1538-1554)

Husband of Lady Jane Grey

He was never king, but he wanted to be, and might well have been king if the Duke of Northumberland's plot to crown Lady Jane Grey had succeeded.

The whole point of Northumberland's plot was to make his own son, Guilford Dudley, King of England. He married Jane to Guilford just six weeks before Edward VI died. Guilford knew what was intended, but Jane herself had no idea of what was afoot.

When the plot failed and Mary took her rightful place on the throne she recognised that both Jane and Guilford Dudley posed a Protestant threat, so after months of imprisonment Guilford was beheaded. In a wheelbarrow his bleeding corpse was trundled past Jane's window in the Tower of London, just before she, too, was led out for execution.

Philip of Spain (1527-1598)

Husband and King Consort of Mary I

Philip was still only a Prince when he came to England to marry Queen Mary, but just before the wedding ceremony began in Winchester Cathedral a herald announced to all those assembled that Philip's father, the Emperor Charles, had just created Philip King of Naples. Thus a King would be marrying a Queen and there would be no disparity in rank.

He was given the title of King of England, but had no power.

Mary was infatuated with him. For her, it did not matter that there was an eleven-year age gap between them.

But Philip had no time for England or his wife. He left after fourteen months. He had been married before, and when news of Mary's death reached him he married twice again.

He sent his heavy fleet of ships, the Armada, to try to invade England but his defeat was total. He did not enjoy a happy relationship with England.

Anne of Denmark (1574-1619)

Wife of James I

James travelled to Oslo in 1590 to marry Anne and when he brought her home it was to Edinburgh, for although he was King James VI of Scotland he was not yet King James I of England. It was thirteen years before the pair were invited south to become the King and Queen of England.

It must have been a welcome change of lifestyle, for it had been a poor and bleak court in Edinburgh.

It was the London of Ben Jonson and Inigo Jones – innovators in staging glittering new forms of courtly entertainment, so for a while they enjoyed a comfortable time.

However, Anne had her share of unhappiness. Several of her children died, and the death of her son Henry, aged 18 and heir to the throne, caused her particular grief. Then her later years were clouded by her husband's crude ways. He was overtly homosexual and never washed.

She insisted on dying in a Danish bed she had imported. It must have reminded her of happier days.

Henrietta Maria (1609-1669)

Wife of Charles I

Daughter of the King of France, lively, haughty, petulant, self-willed, graceful, beautiful. And fiercely Catholic.

She was fifteen when she arrived in England, having already been married by proxy to Charles I in Notre Dame in Paris. Charles married her again in person, in Canterbury Cathedral.

Preparations were in hand for her coronation, but then she dug her heels in and absolutely refused to be crowned by a Protestant. There were violent rows. She even smashed window panes with her bare fists. She refused not merely to be crowned but even to be present.

It was a bad beginning, and the relationship between Charles and Henrietta was cool for a number of years. It was only after Charles's favourite, the Duke of Buckingham, was assassinated that they drew closer together.

The trouble then was that she was continually giving Charles unwanted and bad advice. She hated Parliament and encouraged Charles to ignore it and rule as a king should, by himself. It was a disastrous path to follow . . .

She never witnessed his execution. She had already fled to France. And when Cardinal de Retz visited her to tell her of her husband's death he found her in a desperate state of poverty. In vain she asked Cromwell for an allowance. He sent word back that as she hadn't been crowned, she wasn't properly a queen at all, and so had no claim on the public purse.

She lived to see her son Charles restored to the throne, but she was above all a Princess of France and was buried at St Denis, just outside Paris.

Catherine of Braganza (1638-1705)

Wife of Charles II

Everyone knows about Charles II and his mistresses, but few even remember who his wife was. It was Catherine, a 23-year-old Princess of Portugal. A political marriage, it helped to line up Portugal and Spain against France.

Catherine had to put up with all her husband's concubines and bastards and simply had to swallow her pride. Humiliated, suffering ill-health and not bearing any children, she is probably one of the least known English Queens.

She knew she had been a disappointment to Charles and sent word to beg his forgiveness as he lay dying. "She ask my pardon?" exclaimed Charles. "Alas, poor woman! I beg hers with all my heart."

After Charles's death she returned to Portugal and is buried in Lisbon.

Anne Hyde (1658-1718)

First wife of James II (before he became King)

Anne was the daughter of a clever lawyer, a Mr Hyde, who had been created Earl of Clarendon after his period as Lord Chancellor. James had made Anne pregnant, but despite their difference in rank he married her and two of their daughters were destined to become Queens of England: Mary II and Anne. She died in 1671, aged 34.

Mary of Modena (1658-1718)

Second wife of James II

James II's first wife had been Anne Hyde, by whom he had six children, including the future Queens Mary II and Anne. But his first wife had died and he married a daughter of a north Italian Duke, Mary of Modena.

It was a curious situation. Mary was a fifteen-year-old Italian girl; her husband was forty; she had to live with two step-daughters older than she was; all of Charles's mistresses; and for a while Charles's widowed Portuguese queen, who demanded tactful handling. Added to this, she was unpopular and had to face hostile mobs just because she was Catholic.

The people's worst fears were realised when she gave birth to a son. Rumour spread that she hadn't been pregnant at all and that she had smuggled the baby boy into the palace in a warming-pan so that he could grow up and become a Catholic King.

Revolution burst around her. She disguised herself as a washerwoman and fled with her baby to join James in France.

Prince George of Denmark (1653-1708)

Husband of Queen Anne

George was loyal, faithful to his wife, possessed a huge appetite, drank like a fish, and was unutterably dull and stupid. "I've tried him drunk," said Charles II, "and I've tried him sober – but oddsfish! There's nothing in him!"

The trouble was, there was nothing for him to do. His conversation was nil. On hearing any news, good or bad, his usual remark was "Est-il possible?", and eventually "Est-il possible" became his nickname.

He died six years before Anne, and was buried in Westminster Abbey.

Sophia Dorothea of Zelle (1666-1726)

Divorced wife of George I

Sophia Dorothea was never queen nor did she ever come to England. George had already divorced her for planning to elope with a lover.

Her story is a tragic one. She was only sixteen when she was forced to marry her 22-year-old cousin George, and she hated him from the moment they met. The dislike was mutual; nevertheless, they did have two children, a boy and a girl, and the boy became our George II.

She secretly fell in love with a Swedish count, Philip Konigsmarck, but unfortunately for her, their plans to elope were discovered.

Aged 22 she was sent to prison in the castle of Ahlden in Germany, where she remained until her death thirty-two years later.

She was allowed an eight-mile walk every afternoon, always on the same road. She was sixty when she died, just a year before George.

Caroline of Ansbach (1683-1737)

Wife of George II

She had married George in 1705 when they were both aged twenty-two, and it was to be another twenty-two years before they were to be crowned King and Queen in Westminster Abbey. At the time of their marriage neither of them had any idea that the thrones of Great Britain would be theirs.

Caroline was a good queen, encouraging the arts, including the newest one in her time – gardening. We are indebted to her not only for work on the gardens at Kew but also the completion of Kensington Gardens.

She had waters diverted so that the Serpentine could be made. Her royal gardener was Charles Bridgeman, who invented the 'ha-ha' (a kind of sunken barrier) and who paved the way for Capability Brown.

Despite his many mistresses her husband George II loved and respected her. As she lay dying she begged him to marry again after her death, but the old king told her he couldn't think of it. He told her he'd simply have mistresses instead.

George himself ordered that one side of his own coffin should be taken out, so that he could lie closer to her in death. It was a loving but macabre gesture.

Charlotte of Mecklenburg-Strelitz (1744-1818)

Wife of George III

She was certainly no beauty. She had such a wide mouth that everyone called her the Crocodile. However, George's 17-year-old German bride proved quite fertile. Within less than a year she had produced an heir to the throne – the future George IV – and then, almost annually, there followed an astonishingly numerous succession of babies, fifteen in all.

George and Charlotte were probably the most private and domestic of all monarchs. They enjoyed family life in a quiet, modest residence in Kew. They were both popular and were genuinely interested in meeting people.

Charlotte was kind, sensible and tolerant, but increasingly had to bear the difficulties of her husband's mental ill-health and the scandals surrounding her son. She was intelligent, and probably regretted that she was never allowed to have any part in public affairs.

She died just two years before George, after a marriage of fifty-seven years.

Caroline of Brunswick (1768-1821)

Wife of George IV

When Caroline came to England in 1795 to marry her cousin George he had no desire whatever for a wife: he had a range of mistresses and a wife whom he had married in secret, Mrs Fitzherbert.

However, Parliament was insisting that he should do his duty and provide the country with an heir. They picked Caroline, but no one had the courage to tell George that she was ugly, had bad manners, loose morals, rotten teeth and bad breath. When he met her George gasped: "Pray get me a glass of brandy!" He gulped it down and fled from the room.

Things went from bad to worse. The marriage was consummated, and Caroline had a daughter, but George and Caroline lived together only briefly and then separated.

Her scandalous lifestyle was the subject of an official enquiry, and was a continual embarrassment to everybody. Once, when in Italy, she caused horrified amusement by dancing topless.

George banned her from Westminster Abbey at his coronation and the crowd hooted and jeered at her as she tried in vain to gain entry.

Nineteen days later she died and her body was shipped back to Brunswick.

UNCROWNED QUEENS AND KINGS

Caroline of Brunswick was not the only uncrowned queen. Others were: Margaret of France, second wife of King Edward I.

Jane Seymour, third wife of Henry VIII, who had her coronation postponed because of the plague, and then died shortly after childbirth.

Anne of Cleves, Henry VIII's fourth wife, was never crowned. Lacking the necessary attractions, she was regarded merely as his 'sister'.

Catherine Howard, Henry VIII's fifth wife, executed after 18 months.

Catherine Parr, Henry VIII's sixth wife, was never crowned.

Sophia Dorothea, George I's divorced wife: imprisoned throughout his reign.

Also three reigning monarchs who have never been crowned:

Matilda, 'Lady of the English' in 1141, during King Stephen's reign.

King Edward V, who disappeared, probably murdered in the Tower of London.

King Edward VIII, later Duke of Windsor, who abdicated after reigning 326 days.

Adelaide of Saxe-Meiningen (1792-1849)

Wife of William IV

No princess entered England with less fuss or ceremony. William hated any kind of formality. They were married quietly in a private room at Kew Palace where an old toilet-table was draped over and turned into an altar. Then there was an outdoor family picnic. It was a genuinely happy occasion.

Adelaide was a perfect consort in difficult circumstances. She was tolerant and kind and provided a welcome air of respectability to the court after the scandalous times of George IV. The only sadness was that she failed to provide William with an heir: only two baby daughters who died in infancy.

After William died she enjoyed the freedom to travel and gave money to build the Anglican Cathedral in Valetta, Malta. She has no memorial, but her name is vigorously alive in Australia, where the beautiful city of Adelaide was designed and founded in her honour while she was still queen.

Prince Albert of Saxe-Coburg-Gotha

(1819-1861)

Husband of Queen Victoria

Victoria and Albert were both twenty when they were married: both of them deeply in love. Victoria wrote: "He is perfection in every way – in beauty, in everything . . . Oh, how I adore and love him . . ." And it is true to say that she felt the same about him for the rest of her life.

He was her cousin, coming from Bavaria. Studious, intellectual, humourless. Stiff, earnest, hardworking. His personal motto: "Never relax, never relax, never relax."

It is easy to poke fun at people who treat everything with deadly seriousness, so although Albert worked himself to death on a large number of projects, the English never had much time for him. He was too clever and cultured.

His main achievement was in being the inspirational force behind the Great Exhibition of 1851, by far the largest gathering of arts, sciences, skills and industry which the world had ever seen. It was a triumph of organisation and gave an enormous boost to British commerce. The profits went to form the various museums which are still main tourist attractions in London today. The Albert Hall was also built out of these projects.

He helped design Balmoral and Osborne House; he painted, composed, drew up plans for workers' dwellings; sat on committees; made speeches. He was Albert the Good.

His early death from typhoid fever at the age of 42 plunged Victoria into a lifetime of mourning. No one in public life has ever mourned a spouse so dramatically or so permanently. She lived as a recluse; never went to a theatre or concert; she slept with his nightclothes and always kept a marble model of his 'sweet little ear' on her writing-desk.

The Albert Memorial just opposite the Albert Hall, is the public edifice in his memory, but his grave is a private one, in the Royal Mausoleum at Frogmore, a secluded part of Windsor Park.

It can be claimed that Albert's death influenced the country at least as much as his life. For decades a pall of silence and hushed respectability fell over the English court. No greater contrast could be imagined between the hoots of derision which had been hurled at the licentious George IV and the reverential awe enjoyed by Victoria in her later widowhood.

Alexandra of Denmark (1844-1925)

Wife of Edward VII

Queen Victoria considered Alexandra to be 'one of those sweet creatures who seem to come from the skies to help and bless poor mortals.' She had to be, to marry Edward.

For the first forty years of their marriage, they were the Prince and Princess of Wales. It was a long wait to reach the throne, and Queen Victoria resolutely refused to give Bertie (as Edward was known) any kind of responsibility or work of any kind.

The frustration must have been intense, and he sought every kind of extravagant pleasure, simply to keep himself occupied: racing, hunting, eating, gambling, drinking, travelling, and naturally enough, women.

Alexandra was monumentally tolerant. Gracious and kind, she suffered various health difficulties, especially deafness and lameness, but she kept her strikingly beautiful looks to the end of her life. Everyone knew how unfaithful Bertie was, but she kept a silent dignity and accompanied him without complaint. She was a byword for regal conscientiousness.

Prince Albert had begun the modern royal tradition of service to the community, which we take for granted nowadays. However, this concept of monarchy is a recent innovation, and Alexandra was the first consort queen to involve herself deeply and sincerely in charitable works since those mediaeval queens who retired to nunneries.

She started up a special branch of a military nursing service; she supported hospitals and the International Red Cross; she visited quite ordinary people in their sick-beds. And in 1913, to mark the fiftieth anniversary of her arrival in England, she founded 'Alexandra Rose Day' to support work in hospitals.

To the end of his days Edward was a glutton and a womaniser. When his health finally collapsed he was in Biarritz, accompanied by his long-standing mistress, Mrs Alice Keppel. He was brought home, and when it was evident that he was soon to die, Alexandra, with quite extraordinary selflessness, invited Mrs Keppel to his death-bed to take her last farewell.

Alexandra herself lived on until 1925 and died just before her eighty-first birthday. She has a beautiful memorial next to that of Edward in St. George's Chapel, Windsor.

Mary of Teck (1867-1953)

Wife of George V

Many older people today can still remember the majestic, queenly figure of Queen Elizabeth II's grandmother, Queen Mary. She was almost eight-six when she died, a living link with the past, for when she was born Queen Victoria was still in the first half of her reign, Dickens and George Eliot were still writing and Gladstone and Disraeli were in their prime.

She was born in Kensington Palace, in the same room where Queen Victoria had also been born, and was a great-granddaughter of George III. Her father was Duke Franz of Teck, but May, as she was known, was brought up in England.

Like Catherine of Aragon she was intended in marriage to an heir to the throne who died, but then went on to marry the younger brother and became his queen instead. In this case she was engaged first to a Prince Albert, and then when he died she married Albert's brother George, later to become George V.

She was an exemplary consort. Together they presented an image of rock solid respectability. Duty, courage, faithfulness: all the traditional virtues. During the First World War they did their utmost to set an example, and George even changed his name so that they should not seem German. The name of Windsor was adopted.

After the war there were many social changes, and Mary continued to work for many charities; helped to beautify London's parks; and with her artistic knowledge was a major influence in restoring Buckingham Palace, which had been badly neglected during Victoria's long absence from it.

Her final years were darkened by the abdication of her eldest son, Edward VIII, the death of her youngest son, the Duke of Kent, in a plane crash, and the death from cancer of her middle son, George VI.

Her official memorial is in St George's Chapel, Windsor, but her intangible memorial is the great tradition of duty and service which she personally instilled into her granddaughter, Elizabeth II. She took Elizabeth as a child to concerts, exhibitions and important historical places and helped to bring her up knowing the stories of her ancestors.

She died only a few weeks before Elizabeth's coronation.

Mrs Wallis Simpson (1896-1986)

Duchess of Windsor wife of the Duke of Windsor, formerly King Edward VIII

Edward VIII gave up the throne to marry Wallis Simpson, an American who had already been divorced once and was preparing to divorce a second husband. She mesmerised Edward from the moment they met, at a house party in 1931.

After the abdication Edward was styled 'His Royal Highness the Duke of Windsor' but the honour of being a 'Royal Highness' was pointedly withheld from Wallis when she married him. It rankled deeply.

Nevertheless a tribute came from Adolf Hitler, with whom they once had tea. "She would have made a good Queen," he said. It was a solitary opinion.

SOME FAMOUS MISTRESSES OF ENGLISH KINGS

King Harold	*Edith of the Swan Neck*
Henry II	*The 'Fair Rosamund'*
Edward III	*Alice Perrers*
Edward IV	*Elizabeth Shore, Elizabeth Lucy*
Henry VIII	*Lady Anne Hastings, Jane Popicourt, Elizabeth Blount, Mary Boleyn, Anne Shelton*
Charles II	*Lucy Walter, Barbara Palmer, Hortense Mancini, Louise de Keroualle, Nell Gwynne, and many more*
James II	*Godotha Price, Lady Elizabeth Denham, Arabella Churchill (five bastards by her), Catherine Sedley*
George I	*Sophia von Kilmansegge ('The Elephant'), and Ermengarda Melusina von Schulenburg ('The Maypole')*
George II	*Henrietta Howard, Amelia Sophia von Walmoden*
George IV	*Mary Robinson ('Perdita'), Maria Fitzherbert, many more*
William IV	*Dorothy Jordan (ten children by her)*
Edward VII	*Lillie Langtry, Mrs Keppel, and many more*

Queen Elizabeth the Queen Mother

(born 1900)

Wife of George VI and mother of Queen Elizabeth II

She was born Lady Elizabeth Bowes-Lyon, and can trace descent from the Scottish King Robert II. However, her mother was English and she was born in England. At first she was reluctant to marry the Duke of York (as George VI then was), saying that she feared "I should never again be free to think, speak or act as I really feel I should think, speak and act." In fact she only accepted him on his third proposal.

Photographs at the time show just how beautiful she was, and anecdotes recall how she charmed away the stuffiness of the royal family.

In the ordinary course of events she would have been just a relatively minor member of the royal family, hardly worth a footnote in history, but the abdication of Edward VIII pitchforked the Duke and herself into positions neither of them wanted. The Duke was horrified at the prospect of becoming King, but Elizabeth provided support in a manner equalled by no other queen.

Throughout the war they stayed in London, sharing the dangers of the blitz. When Buckingham Palace itself was bombed, Elizabeth remarked: "Now I feel I can look the East End in the face." It was a typical reaction.

Day after day George and Elizabeth toured the scenes of devastation. People will never forget that sympathy, that common bond. Victory came, but also the years of austerity, and then widowhood.

It would have been easy for her to retire into obscurity, and this she was tempted to do. But her vitality, her love of family, her sense of duty and her sheer *joie de vivre* gradually returned. She became more involved in public service than ever before, becoming president, patron, Colonel-in-Chief, or whatever, of well over three hundred organisations who look to her for inspiration and support.

She holds the record of being the longest-living monarch or consort, and even the most savage critic of royalty has to remain silent in the face of her outstanding contribution to public life.

Someone once wrote of her as being a "marsh-mallow with a core of good Scotch granite".

Charm is always there, but it is the granite which we respect and love.

Prince Philip, Duke of Edinburgh

(Born 1921)

Husband of Queen Elizabeth II

Philip was born a prince of Greece. His father, who died in 1944, was Prince Andrew of Greece, and his mother was Princess Alice, a great granddaughter of Queen Victoria. However, his ancestry is pure Danish and he does not have a drop of Greek blood in his veins.

When he was eighteen, a naval cadet at Dartmouth, he was allowed to meet the young Princess Elizabeth, then aged 13, owing to their distant kinship, and from that moment Elizabeth never had eyes for any other boy. That may sound like a tinsel fairy-tale, but it is the factual truth.

King George VI was worried that his daughter had simply fallen for the first boy she had met, and tried his hardest to delay an engagement. But Elizabeth had made up her mind. In 1946 they were engaged and in 1947 they were married.

Elizabeth and Philip were to enjoy only just over four years of freedom before they had to take over the roles of Queen and Consort.

Philip had set his mind on a naval career, but the death of George VI in mid-life cut short any hopes for this. Instead, he has been active, incredibly active, in travelling, speaking, sponsoring.

He is the president, patron, Colonel-in-Chief, chancellor, chairman, governor, admiral, ranger, general commander-in-chief, captain-general, chief, trust member, etc. of close on six hundred organisations.

In addition to accompanying the Queen on her innumerable tours, he has undertaken a vast number of independent trips by himself. It has been calculated that he works a fourteen-hour day, travels an average of 75,000 miles a year, carries out about 300 engagements and makes about 80 speeches a year.

His most lasting innovation has been his Duke of Edinburgh Award Scheme, which has given personal challenges to well over a million youngsters not only in Great Britain but also in the twenty-five Commonwealth countries around the world.

Detractors of the monarchy should pause to consider this aspect of voluntary public service now carried out by most of the royals. No previous consort, surely, has been involved so widely in the life of the country as Philip.

CONSORT QUEENS, KINGS AND PRINCES

(Dates given are those of birth and death; age at death; age at marriage)

William I	Matilda of Flanders	c1031-1083	d 52	m 22
Henry I	Matilda of Scotland		d 38	m 20
	Adela of Louvain	1103-1151	d 48	m 18
Stephen	Matilda of Boulogne	1103-1152	d 49	m 22
Henry II	Eleanor of Aquitaine	1122-1204	d 82	m 30
Richard I	Berengaria of Navarre	1165-1230	d 65	m 26
John	Isabella of Angoulême	1186-1246	d 60	m 14
Henry III	Eleanor of Provence	1222-1291	d 69	m 14
Edward I	Eleanor of Castile	1244-1290	d 46	m 10
	Margaret of France	1282-1317	d 35	m 16
Edward II	Isabella of France	1292-1358	d 66	m 16
Edward III	Philippa of Hainault	1314-1369	d 55	m 14
Richard II	Anne of Bohemia	1366-1394	d 28	m 16
	Isabella of Valois	1387-1410	d 23	m 8
Henry IV	Joanne of Navarre	1370-1437	d 67	m 33
Henry V	Catherine of Valois	1401-1437	d 36	m 19
Henry VI	Margaret of Anjou	1430-1482	d 52	m 15
Edward IV	Elizabeth Woodville	1437-1429	d 55	m 27
Richard III	Anne of Warwick	1456-1485	d 29	m 16
Henry VII	Elizabeth of York	1466-1503	d 37	m 20
Henry VIII	Catherine of Aragon	1486-1536	d 37	m 23
	Anne Boleyn	1507-1536	d 29	m 26
	Jane Seymour	1506-1537	d 31	m 30
	Anne of Cleves	1515-1557	d 42	m 25
	Catherine Howard	1522-1542	d 20	m 18
	Catherine Parr	1512-1548	d 36	m 31
Jane	Lord Guilford Dudley	1538-1554	d 16	m 15
Mary I	Philip of Spain	1527-1598	d 71	m 27
James I	Anne of Denmark	1574-1619	d 45	m 15
Charles I	Henrietta Maria	1609-1669	d 60	m 16
Charles II	Catherine of Braganza	1638-1705	d 67	m 23
James II	Mary of Modena	1658-1718	d 60	m 15
Anne	George of Denmark	1665-1714	d 49	m 18
George I	Sophia of Zelle	1666-1726	d 60	m 16
George II	Caroline of Ansbach	1683-1737	d 54	m 22
George III	Charlotte of Mecklenburg-Strelitz	1744-1818	d 74	m 17
George IV	Caroline of Brunswick	1768-1821	d 53	m 27
William IV	Adelaide of Saxe-Meiningen	1792-1849	d 57	m 26
Victoria	Albert of Saxe-Coburg-Gotha	1819-1861	d 41	m 21
Edward VII	Alexandra of Denmark	1844-1925	d 81	m 19
George V	Mary of Teck	1867-1953	d 81	m 19
Edward VIII	(Mrs Wallis Simpson)	1896-1986	d 90	m 41
George VI	Elizabeth Bowes-Lyon	1900 -		m 23
Elizabeth II	Prince Philip of Greece	1921 -		m 26

A SHORT GAZETTEER OF PLACES OF ROYAL INTEREST

Clearly it would be impossible to list every house, town or castle which has been visited by monarchs over the last fifteen hundred years. However, here is a selected list of places which are of particular royal interest.

Overseas visitors, we hope, will find this short-list helpful when they plan their holidays. On pages 150-151 you will find some useful telephone numbers which will enable you to contact many of these places and check when they are open to the public.

ALNWICK CASTLE

Alnwick Castle, home of the Dukes of Northumberland, is about 33 miles north of Newcastle.

At one time it was a stronghold of the Percy family (see Shakespeare's *Henry IV*). Malcolm III of Scotland was killed here in November 1093, as he was attempting his fifth invasion of England. And in July 1174 William I of Scotland (William the Lion) was captured here.

Another home of the Dukes of Northumberland is Syon House, near Kew on the outskirts of London. It was John Dudley, Duke of Northumberland, who was 'Lord Protector' of King Edward VI, and who tried unsuccessfully to put Lady Jane Grey on the throne. (See ***Syon House***).

ALTHORP

This country house is about 6 miles north of Northampton, and was the home of the 8th Earl of Spencer, father of Diana, Princess of Wales.

ARUNDEL CASTLE

This imposing castle, about 10 miles east of Chichester, is the home of the Dukes of Norfolk. It has had a long history, and was originally the home of Adela, the second wife of Henry I. The Empress Matilda was besieged here by King Stephen.

The castle is much altered from those days, but over its long history it has been visited by many monarchs, including Victoria and Albert and Elizabeth II.

ASCOT

The race-course, at Ascot Heath in Berkshire, was laid out by order of Queen Anne in 1711, who began the Royal Ascot Races.

Nowadays this is an annual fashionable four-day race-meeting held in June, usually attended by royalty.

AUDLEY END HOUSE

About sixteen miles south of Cambridge, this is a large country house with many royal connections. James I was entertained here, and Charles II bought it and treated it as his summer holiday home, coming here regularly.

The house reverted to its former owners, the Earls of Suffolk, in the 18th century.

BALMORAL CASTLE

This is a private residence of the monarch, about 50 miles west of Aberdeen on the River Dee. Queen Victoria fell in love with the place, and she and Prince Albert bought the estate in 1844.

Prince Albert collaborated with a local architect to design and build the present 'Scottish baronial' castle. It is the most private and secluded of all the royal residences.

BAMBURGH CASTLE

On the Northumberland coast, about 46 miles north of Newcastle-on-Tyne. It was a stronghold against Danish invaders and against the Scots. Associated with the Northumbrian King and Saint, Oswald I. William Rufus besieged the castle when Robert de Mowbray attempted a rebellion.

Many other mediaeval kings stayed here when in the north, and it served as a Lancastrian stronghold in the Wars of the Roses. Henry VI lived here for nine months.

BANQUETING HOUSE

Whitehall, London. It is easy to miss this as you walk up Whitehall from the Houses of Parliament to Trafalgar Square, but it has immense historical importance. It is the only surviving part of a new Palace of Whitehall, begun by Inigo Jones for James I in 1619.

It heralded the coming of classical architecture to England. It was from this building that Charles I walked to the scaffold outside, to be beheaded.

BATH

This cathedral city, about 12 miles south-east of Bristol, is filled with royal connections. The Saxon King Edgar was crowned here in 973, and many kings and queens have visited the city and enjoyed the warm baths there, originally developed by the Romans.

King John is believed to have been the first sovereign to take the warm waters of the King's Bath. Later monarchs include Henry VI (who found the baths dirty!), Charles I, Charles II and James II, who 'touched for the King's Evil' in a Roman Catholic rite in Bath Abbey.

The hey-day of Bath's fortunes was in the eighteenth century, and the future George IV added royal distinction when he visited the city in 1796 and 1799.

BEAULIEU ABBEY

Hampshire, 14 miles south of Southampton. Nowadays Beaulieu has many modern attractions, including the famous Motor Museum. Its abbey was visited by several monarchs, including Henry III, Henry VI and Henry VII, but after the Dissolution of the Monasteries the abbey was converted into a residence by Thomas Wriothesley, Earl of Southampton.

James I frequently stayed here as guest of the 3rd Earl. Edward VII and Kaiser Wilhelm II came here in 1907.

BELVOIR CASTLE

Leicestershire, 7 miles south-west of Grantham. Home of the Dukes of Rutland. Many royal visitors have stayed here. The old Belvoir castle was destroyed by Cromwell and the present building dates from the 18th century.

The Prince Regent gourmandised here in 1814 (he ate and drank so much that he had to be 'bled'). Queen Victoria and Albert were here in 1843.

BERKELEY CASTLE

Gloucestershire, about 10 miles south-west of Stroud. There are many royal connections, but the most famous event was the cruel murder of Edward II, which took place here in 1327.

BLENHEIM PALACE

Woodstock, about 9 miles north of Oxford. Not a royal palace, although it is one of the finest palaces in the country. Begun in 1705, it was built for John Churchill, first Duke of Marlborough, in gratitude for his victory at Blenheim.

Most sovereigns have visited Blenheim since then, and Winston Churchill was born here. In earlier times Woodstock was the site of earlier royal homes, including that of Henry II's mistress, the 'Fair Rosamund'.

BLICKLING HALL

Norfolk, about 15 miles north of Norwich. The present mansion was built in the early 17th century and Charles II and his queen, Catherine of Braganza, were guests here.

But an earlier mansion on the same site belonged to the Boleyn family and tradition has it that Anne Boleyn spent her childhood holidays there. Her ghost is said to haunt the site still.

BOGNOR REGIS

It was George V who allowed the 'Regis' part of its name to be added, after he had spent a period of convalescence there. When the king was told of the municipal authorities' request, he is quoted as having irritably muttered 'Bugger Bognor!'

Lord Stamfordham is said to have conveyed a more tactful version of the reply to the waiting deputation, saying that His Majesty would be graciously pleased to grant their request.

BOLINGBROKE CASTLE

In Old Bolingbroke, Lincolnshire, about 26 miles east of Lincoln. It was the birthplace of the usurper King Henry IV, known before his reign as Henry Bolingbroke. It is little more than a ruin now.

BOSCOBEL HOUSE

Shropshire, 4 miles east of Tong. This was a royalist refuge during the Civil War and Charles II spent a day hiding in an oak tree on the estate after the Battle of Worcester. A descendant of the original tree is still to be seen.

BOSWORTH FIELD

Leicestershire, about 2 miles south of Market Bosworth. The site of the important Battle of Bosworth, 1485, in which the last of the Plantagenets, Richard III, was defeated and killed, and after which Henry Tudor succeeded to the throne as Henry VII.

The site is beautifully laid out now, with clear explanations of how the course of the battle unfolded. A visitor centre adds greatly to an understanding of this momentous event.

BRADGATE PARK

Leicestershire, about 7 miles north-west of Leicester. Bradgate Manor was the birthplace in 1537 of Lady Jane Grey, the 'Nine Days' Queen'. She was brought up here and became a notable linguist and scholar despite her young age.

The house is now no longer more than a collection of ruins, but there are 1,250 acres of park, within Charnwood Forest, open to the public throughout the year. Deer can be seen in the beautiful surrounding woodland.

BRIGHTON PAVILION

Briefly, Charles II came to the little coastal fishing village of 'Brighthelmstone' on his last night in England before escaping to France after the Battle of Worcester in 1651. He little knew that this village would turn into a royal holiday resort where a future monarch would build one of the most extravagantly ornamented 'palaces' in the kingdom.

Brighton Pavilion is essential viewing for a tourist wanting to understand the world of 'Prinny' – the Prince Regent and future King George IV. Several of Prinny's uncles, including 'Butcher' Cumberland, had enjoyed the new cult of sea-bathing in Brighton, and when Prinny came in 1783 he liked the area so much that he came here regularly for almost the rest of his life, installing his secret wife, Mrs Maria Fitzherbert here.

He took an old farmhouse and turned it first into a classical villa, and then, during this Regency period, his architect, John Nash, transformed it into the astonishing building we know today as Brighton Pavilion, with its onion-shaped dome, tent-shaped roofs, minarets, and elaborate riot of decoration – Indian, Arabian, Turkish, Chinese: every conceivable exotic style.

George IV's brother, William IV, also spent time here and added extra lodges to the Pavilion for his wife, but Queen Victoria disliked the place, closed it, and the town of Brighton bought it in 1850.

After a recent fire, it has now been brilliantly restored, and glows with vibrant colour. It is probably in better condition now than it has ever been.

Brighton is on the Sussex coast, only an hour from London. Prinny himself once commuted to London – but as trains weren't invented at the time (1784) he did it on horseback – a return journey of ten hours.

BUCKINGHAM PALACE

The surprising fact about Buckingham Palace is just how relatively recently it has become the central focus of royalty in London. Queen Victoria was the first monarch to live there, but she virtually abandoned it after the death of her husband Prince Albert. Her son, Edward VII, was born there in 1841 and died there in 1910; and Prince Charles was born there in 1948.

Before it became the huge palace it is today, it was a comparatively modest town house, belonging to John Sheffield, Duke of Buckingham. King George III first bought 'Buckingham House', as it was then called, in 1762, and extended it to house his growing family and large library.

During this period it was known as the 'Queen's House' and Queen Charlotte gave birth to twelve of her fifteen children there, including the future King William IV.

It is to George IV and his grandiose architectural ambitions that we owe the present Buckingham Palace. He was fifty-eight when he came to the throne in 1820, living at the time in Carlton House, at the east end of the Mall. He decided that he needed a much more elaborate palace, and entrusted the enlargement of Buckingham House to his favourite architect, John Nash.

Parliament was horrified at the expense, which grew more and more as Nash's plans were implemented. Work began in 1825 and the palace was not quite completed when George IV died in 1830.

William IV disliked the place, and never lived there. When the Houses of Parliament were burnt down in 1835 William even suggested that Buckingham Palace would make a good substitute.

Queen Victoria, however, moved in almost immediately after her accession, and it was under her direction that further enlargement took place. The railings around the front court were not erected until 1906.

The Mall was widened and the Victoria Memorial was unveiled by George V in 1911, and it was not until 1912 that the final work on the front of the palace was eventually completed.

The ceremony of Changing the Guard takes place daily at 11.30. The public may visit the Queen's Gallery in Buckingham Palace Road, in which selections from the royal art collections are constantly rotated.

The Royal Mews is also open to visitors. And in recent years Buckingham Palace itself has been open to the public during the summer months. It is an experience not to be missed.

BURY ST EDMUNDS

The name of this cathedral city in Suffolk means just what it says: it is where St Edmund was buried. He was King of East Anglia, defeated and killed by Danish invaders in 870. He became venerated as a martyr, and his shrine became a place of pilgrimage. Nowadays the shrine is no more. However, it is worth remembering that St Edmund was a predecessor of St George as England's patron saint. Later on, St Edward the Confessor took his place, and later still St George supplanted them both.

CAERNARVON CASTLE

Wales. Built by Edward I, begun in 1283. Edward I's son, Edward II, was invested as the first Prince of Wales here, and Prince Charles was invested as Prince of Wales here in 1969.

CAMBRIDGE

This famous university city is about 60 miles north of London. Many Kings and Queens have visited it, but certainly the pride of place in terms of world fame must be given to King's College, founded by King Henry VI. He laid the foundation stone of its beautiful chapel in 1446. His queen, Margaret of Anjou, founded Queens' College, situated next to it.

A visitor to King's College Chapel will be immediately struck by the Tudor emblems which are to be found everywhere. It was left to the Tudor Henry VIII to complete the building. Interestingly, on the wooden choir-screen, there are several carvings of 'H' and 'A' – showing that it was made in that very short period when Henry was married to Anne Boleyn (1533-36).

Similarly, Queens' College was refounded and completed by Elizabeth Woodville, queen to Edward IV. Hence two queens were responsible for its foundation, and the correct positioning of the apostrophe after the 's' in Queens' is crucially important!

Other colleges with royal connections are Trinity College, founded by King Henry VIII; and St John's College and Christ's College, both founded by Lady Margaret Beaufort, mother of King Henry VII.

During the Civil War Cambridge was generally in favour of the Parliamentarians; Oliver Cromwell had been an undergraduate of Sidney Sussex College, and was M.P. for the nearby town of Huntingdon. His head is buried in the chapel of his old college.

Trinity College has the distinction of having had two future kings, Edward VII and George VI, as undergraduates for brief spells: but their attendance was hardly more than a token. Prince Charles, however, also an undergraduate at Trinity, lived the full three years in college working for and gaining his Cambridge degree.

His father, Prince Philip, has been Chancellor of Cambridge University since 1977.

CANTERBURY

This great cathedral city lies about 60 miles south-east of London and about 16 miles north-west of Dover.

Lying as it does so near to the coast, it has been a natural stopping-place for almost every king and queen coming or going to France via Dover.

Crucial to the history of these islands was the arrival from Rome in 597 of St Augustine. He converted and baptised Ethelbert I, ruler of the Saxon Kingdom of Kent, and was given land for an abbey and a cathedral. Since then, Canterbury has been the 'capital city' of the Christian church in England, where the Archbishops have had their seat.

The most notable event in the city's history was the murder of Thomas Becket, Archbishop of Canterbury, within the cathedral itself on 29 December 1170. Becket had quarrelled with the fiery-tempered King Henry II, and four of Henry's knights killed Becket, thinking they were carrying out the king's wishes. In a dramatic show of penitence King Henry walked barefoot through the city, spent the night in prayer, and allowed himself to be solemnly beaten by every cleric present.

During the middle ages Becket's shrine was visited by thousands of pilgrims every year, and the city prospered enormously as a result.

Other royal events included a second coronation for King Stephen, after he had lost power for a while during his conflict with Matilda; the burial of the Black Prince, who specially wished to be laid near Becket's shrine; the burial of King Henry IV and his queen, Joan of Navarre; the marriage of King Charles I to his queen Henrietta Maria; the welcoming back to England of Charles II after his exile; and the meeting of Prince Charles with Pope Paul II in 1982.

Visits to Canterbury by reigning monarchs have been so numerous that they can hardly be listed here. Sufficient to say that Canterbury has been the main meeting-place of royalty and the church for no less than 1400 years.

CARISBROOKE CASTLE

This castle, on the Isle of Wight, is most famous for having been one of the main places of imprisonment of Charles I after his capture at the end of the Civil War.

He stayed here for a year, and was allowed some freedom at first; but as he was continually plotting with his Scottish supporters he lost that freedom and was taken to Hurst Castle and thence to London for trial.

CARLISLE

Only nine miles south of the Scottish border, Carlisle had great strategic importance in the continual struggles between England and Scotland. William Rufus founded the castle here in 1092 and many mediaeval kings came to try to assert their authority there. King Alexander II of Scotland captured Carlisle and its castle in 1216. Edward I of England 'the Hammer of the Scots', made it his headquarters as he planned his campaigns.

Mary, Queen of Scots, lived here for a while in 1568 as she sought refuge in England, the first of a long series of lodgings (Bolton, Tutbury, Wingfield Manor, Coventry, Chatsworth, Sheffield, Buxton, Chartley Hall and Fotheringhay) as she became more and more firmly a prisoner of Queen Elizabeth I.

CARLTON HOUSE

Only the memory remains of 'Prinny's' London palace at the Admiralty Arch end of the Mall. The site is now taken by Carlton House Terrace and Nos. 107-8 Pall Mall. However, the site is worth glancing at and remembering that at one time it held a glittering palace, a forerunner of Buckingham Palace. Regent Street was constructed in order to give the Prince Regent a clear route direct from Carlton House to his new Regent's Park.

However, when Buckingham Palace was begun in 1826, Carlton House was pulled down. Interestingly, eight large stone columns from Carlton House are now still to be seen in the porticoes of the National Gallery in Trafalgar Square.

CASTLE RISING

Norfolk, about 5 miles north-east of King's Lynn. It is a massive ruin. Some of the walls are nine feet thick. Worth a quick visit if you are in this part of England, to see what a typical Norman castle must have been like.

Its link with royalty is that King Edward III kept his mother, Queen Isabella (the 'She-Wolf of France') imprisoned here for 30 years after her part in the murder of his father (Edward II).

CHARLECOTE PARK

Warwickshire, about 4 miles east of Stratford-upon-Avon. A beautiful Elizabethan house with an extensive 'Capability Brown' deer park.

William Shakespeare is said to have got into trouble with the original owner, Sir Thomas Lucy, by poaching his deer. Elizabeth I was entertained here, and Charles I's army camped nearby just before the Battle of Edgehill, 1642.

CHARING CROSS

In the forecourt of the present railway station, overlooking the Strand in central London, is a nineteenth century reproduction of the original 'Eleanor Cross' put up by King Edward I in 1291.

The original cross stood on the site of the statue of King Charles I on horseback, at the top of Whitehall.

CHATSWORTH HOUSE

Derbyshire. One of the greatest historic houses in the country, about ten miles west of Chesterfield. Although it was greatly enlarged in the 17th and 18th centuries, the original house was begun by Sir William Chatsworth, who was Cardinal Wolsey's secretary, and completed by his widow, the famous 'Bess of Hardwick'.

Many royal visitors have stayed here, including Victoria and her consort Albert, who was so impressed by the huge conservatories here that he employed their designer, Joseph Paxton, to become the architect of the Crystal Palace, at his Great Exhibition of 1851.

Mary, Queen of Scots was prisoner-guest here on several occasions.

CHESTER

Cheshire, about 25 miles south of Liverpool. A cathedral city and former headquarters of Roman legionaries. Its proximity to Wales made it a useful base for Edward I's campaigns against the Welsh, and its castle afforded lodging to many other kings and queens.

It is a town filled with royal connections, one of the earliest being the occasion when the Saxon King Edgar was ceremonially rowed on the River Dee by six (or eight) lesser kings – including Malcolm of Strathclyde, Kenneth II of Scotland, and several Welsh kings. Visitors can walk round the top of the impressive city walls and enter the tower from which King Charles I despairingly saw his army vanquished in the battle of Rowton Moor in September 1642.

CLAREMONT HOUSE

Near Esher, Surrey. The house was built in the late 18th century. It was here that Princess Charlotte, daughter of George IV and Caroline of Brunswick, died shortly after childbirth. Victoria loved the place, and often visited her uncle Leopold there.

'Claremont remains as the brightest epoch of my otherwise rather melancholy childhood,' she wrote in later years. The house is sometimes open, and the gardens are open throughout the year.

CLARENCE HOUSE

Close to St James's Palace, London. It is named after the Duke of Clarence, younger brother of George IV, who succeeded him to the throne in 1830 as William IV.

It is still very much a part of royal life: after their marriage Princess Elizabeth and her husband (the future Elizabeth II and the Duke of Edinburgh) lived there for a while, and Princess Anne was born there in 1950. Queen Elizabeth the Queen Mother has lived there since 1952.

CLIVEDEN HOUSE

Buckinghamshire, about 4 miles from Maidenhead. A beautiful mansion and large estate on the bank of the Thames. This is the third house on the site, and was the home of Lady Astor.

However, the first house was the home from 1739 to 1751 of Frederick, Prince of Wales, son of George II, and father of George III. He was a keen gardener and parts of the lovely gardens date from his time. It was here that Frederick was hit by a cricket ball, receiving an injury which ultimately killed him; and it was here that the future King George III was brought up.

COLCHESTER

Essex, about 62 miles north-east of London. The Normans built a massive castle here on foundations which were originally the base of the Roman Temple of Claudius. Even before that it must have been a centre of local British kings. King Coel lived here ('Old King Cole' of the well-known nursery rhyme) whose daughter, if the mediaeval historian Geoffrey of Monmouth is to be believed, was Helena (who later became a saint, and after whom the island of St Helena is named).

And it was Helena's famous son, the Emperor Constantine, who converted the whole of the Roman Empire to Christianity in 324.

There are many royal links and the town and its castle were visited by many kings and queens. It was a royalist stronghold during the Civil War.

CORFE CASTLE

Dorset, about 6 miles west of Swanage. The scene in 978 of the murder of King Edward (saint and martyr) probably on the orders of his stepmother Elfrida. William the Conqueror greatly strengthened the castle. King John was fond of the place and often stayed here.

During the Civil War it was a stronghold of the royalists, defended by Lady Bankes. It surrendered to Cromwell's besieging forces in 1646 and was then 'slighted' – i.e. blown up and reduced to the picturesque ruin it is today.

COVENTRY

West Midlands, about 16 miles south-east of Birmingham. A town of great history and often visited by royalty, but it refused entry to Charles I at the beginning of the Civil War. George VI came within hours to see the devastation after it had been bombed in 1940, and Elizabeth II came to the consecration of the new cathedral in 1962.

COWES

Isle of Wight. Famous for its sailing races. Cowes Regatta has been a major event patronised by royalty ever since the time of George IV.

DARTMOUTH

On the Devon coast about 40 miles south-west of Exeter. Richard I used this port to assemble his fleet for the Holy Land. Modern royals receiving naval training here have been George V, Edward VIII, George VI, Prince Philip, Prince Charles and Prince Andrew.

DERBY

Derbyshire. This cathedral city was the southernmost town reached by Bonnie Prince Charlie (the Jacobite 'Young Pretender') in 1745 as he travelled south from Scotland to attempt to claim the throne. After two days, taking good advice, he went back north.

DOVER

Kent. The nearest port to France, and therefore of immense importance as kings and queens have travelled to and from the continent. William the Conqueror built its massive castle, and virtually every monarch has come here. The story of Dover Castle is the history of England!

DURHAM

County Durham. Cathedral city about 14 miles south of Newcastle. Its castle was built by William the Conqueror, and thus the city, already important because it was the burial-place of St Cuthbert, became of great strategic significance in dealings with the Scots.

The Normans also built the majestic cathedral. Many kings and queens have visited both castle and cathedral.

EDINBURGH

Edinburgh has been the capital of Scotland for over a thousand years. Its Castle dominates the city, and has served as palace, prison, fortress, shrine and arsenal. St. Margaret's Chapel is named for St. Margaret, wife of King Malcolm III of Scotland, grand-daughter of Edmund Ironside and daughter of Edgar the Atheling. (Margaret was one of the last members of the Anglo-Saxon royal family, and she sought refuge in the Scottish court at the time of the Norman Conquest. Her daughter Matilda became the queen of King Henry I of England, see page 83).

Mary Queen of Scots gave birth to James VI of Scotland and I of England in a small room here. Much Scottish royal memorabilia, including the Scottish Regalia (much older than the English) are kept in this fascinating castle.

ETON

Berkshire. A few miles from Windsor. Visitors to Windsor Castle can see Eton college in the distance. It was founded in 1440 by the nineteen-year-old King Henry VI.

The young king was passionately keen on his two great educational projects, Eton College and King's College Cambridge, and he personally designed Eton College chapel and its buildings.

EXETER

Devon. Many royal visitors have come here for various reasons. Charles I's wife, Henrietta Maria, gave birth to their youngest child 'Minette' here. Probably the most exciting visit of a monarch was the arrival of William of Orange in 1688, with an army including 3000 Swiss mercenaries. He was on his way to London to claim the throne.

The Duke of Clarence, (the future King William IV) came here on a number of visits; hence the name of the Royal Clarence Hotel, facing the cathedral.

FALMOUTH

Cornwall. Two queens have passed through this fishing town: Joan of Navarre arrived in 1403 to become the wife of Henry IV; and Henrietta Maria departed in 1644, escaping from the horrors of the Civil War.

FAVERSHAM

Kent, about 10 miles west of Canterbury. King Stephen was buried in an abbey which he founded here. In 1688 an extraordinary scene occurred when James II was brought here, captured by fishermen while he was on a boat off Sheppey and trying to escape from the clutches of William of Orange.

He was brought before magistrates and hustled back to London. Shortly afterwards he managed a more successful escape.

FLODDEN FIELD

Northumberland. The site of the Battle of Flodden, 1513, when the Earl of Surrey defeated a Scottish army. Almost 10,000 Scots were killed, including their king, James IV, grandfather of Mary Queen of Scots and great-grandfather of James VI of Scotland and I of England.

James IV was the last king in Britain to be killed in battle. There is a monument to commemorate the battle.

FOTHERINGHAY

Northamptonshire. A village about 10 miles south-west of Peterborough. it was the site of a Norman castle, and the future King Richard III was born there. It was a favourite royal residence until, in 1586, it became the last place of imprisonment of Mary Queen of Scots.

On 8 February 1587 Mary was beheaded in the Great Hall here. Nothing remains of the building now, except a single piece of masonry and a grassy mound. The local church is worth visiting.

FROGMORE HOUSE

In Windsor Home Park, Berkshire. An eighteenth century mansion used by Queen Charlotte, and later by Queen Victoria's mother.

The Mausoleum in the grounds is the resting-place of Prince Albert and Queen Victoria, and nearby is a private royal cemetery in which the Duke and Duchess of Windsor are buried. The gardens and mausoleum are open only very occasionally.

GEDDINGTON

A tiny village in Northamptonshire, four miles north of Kettering. If you are in this part of the country it is worth taking a detour to see one of the surviving 'Eleanor Crosses'.

Queen Eleanor, wife of Edward I, died at Harby in Nottinghamshire in 1290, and Edward had 12 beautiful crosses set up to mark the twelve places where her body rested on its way to be buried in Westminster Abbey.

GLASTONBURY

Somerset, about 22 miles south-west of Bath. The religious and 'new age' significance of Glastonbury is world-famed. As a place connected with royalty it is to be remembered that three Saxon kings are buried here: Edmund I, Edgar, and Edmund II ('Ironside').

King Arthur's huge bones are said to be buried here too. Henry VI and Henry VII came here on pilgrimage, but Glastonbury Abbey was destroyed with all the others by Henry VIII.

GLOUCESTER

Cathedral city and county town, 103 miles west of London. The town and cathedral have had many royal connections. Edward the Confessor held his court here at Christmas, as did William the Conqueror and William Rufus. It was on one of these occasions that the Conqueror gave orders for the Domesday Book to be compiled. Henry III, as a boy of nine, was given a first coronation here in 1216. The most important royal event, however, was the burial of the murdered Edward II in 1327, and following this Gloucester cathedral became a place of pilgrimage. It supported the Parliamentarians in the Civil War and resisted a royalist siege by Charles II in 1643.

GREENWICH

London. The original palace here was built by Henry V's brother, the Duke of Gloucester, and this became a favourite royal residence in succeeding years. Henry VI recovered from his mental illness here in 1455.

Henry VII converted this into a Tudor palace, and it was in this royal dwelling that Henry VIII was born. Mary I and Elizabeth I were also born here.

The old Tudor palace was also the scene of much history. Anne Boleyn was sent to the Tower from here; Elizabeth I held court here, and was entertained by Shakespeare's company, who staged two plays for her pleasure.

James I gave the palace to his queen, Anne of Denmark, Inigo Jones built a 'House of Delight' for her. It became known as the 'Queen's House', and was used by Henrietta Maria, queen of Charles I.

Charles II demolished the old Tudor palace in order to build a new one, but this was never completed. However, the park was landscaped and it was in his reign that Greenwich Observatory was built. Wren, Hawksmoor and Vanburgh produced the beautiful buildings which we see today.

George I and his son, arrived at Greenwich in 1714 to begin the Hanoverian rule in Great Britain; and Caroline of Brunswick also landed here to marry the future George IV.

In our own time, Queen Elizabeth II knighted Sir Francis Chichester at Greenwich after he had sailed round the world in his ketch, Gipsy Moth IV.

GUILDFORD

Surrey, 30 miles west of London. Remains of a Norman castle and mediaeval royal palace are still to be visited, just off the high street. Many kings enjoyed living here or making stop-over visits.

It was a favourite of Henry III, who had the palace made specially comfortable for the ten-year-old Eleanor of Castile, after she had just married his son, the future Edward I.

The last connection with royalty was in December 1688, when James Edward, the baby Prince of Wales, (the 'Old Pretender') was hidden here after an attempt to smuggle him to France had failed.

HAMPTON COURT PALACE

Greater London, about 3 miles from Kingston-upon-Thames. Every visitor to Great Britain should try to see Hampton Court Palace, built between 1514 and 1530 for Cardinal Wolsey, but then given by him to Henry VIII in a vain attempt to win back royal favour.

Over the next two and a quarter centuries all Britain's kings and queens lived here and many additions have been made to the original Tudor palace.

Upon taking possession, Henry VIII added the Great Hall, a new kitchen, a tilt-yard and the real-tennis court. it was here that he fêted Anne Boleyn; here that Jane Seymour gave birth to the future Edward VI and shortly afterwards died; here that Henry lived briefly with Anne of Cleves; here that he adored Catherine Howard until he heard of her infidelities;here that he married Catherine Parr, his sixth and final wife.

Mary I and her husband Philip of Spain lived here, as did Elizabeth I, James I, Charles I, and Oliver Cromwell, governing England as Lord Protector.

Charles II brought his mistresses here. It was the favourite residence of William and Mary, who redecorated it, and it was while riding to Hampton Court from Kensington that William fell and received his fatal injuries.

Queen Anne gave birth to her longest-living son, the Duke of Gloucester, at Hampton Court.

George I and George II both lived here, but one day George II lost his temper with his grandson, the future George III and boxed his ears. Perhaps the effect of this was to make George III dislike Hampton Court, for after he became king in 1760 he never even visited the place again, nor has any sovereign lived here since that time.

A part of Hampton Court Palace was damaged by fire in 1986 but it has now been fully restored. There is so much to see here that half a day is hardly enough: there are six separate routes to take: Henry VIII's State Apartments; the Queen's Apartments; the Georgian Rooms; the King's Apartments; the Wolsey Rooms and Renaissance Picture Gallery; and the Tudor Kitchens.

If you have energy after all this, there are sixty acres of Palace Gardens to see – Tudor, Baroque and Victorian – laid out by generations of royal gardeners; a greenhouse containing the largest and oldest vine in the world, planted in 1768; and you can always get lost in the Maze, set out by the gardeners of William III's reign in the 1690s.

HATFIELD HOUSE

Hertfordshire, 21 miles north of London. Henry VIII bought the mediaeval manor here and used it as a separate residence for his daughter, the future Elizabeth I. Elizabeth spent a great deal of her childhood at Hatfield and in 1558 she heard of the death of her half-sister Mary and realised that she had then become Queen. She held her first Council in the Hall here.

Many royal relics articles remain here: splendid portraits of Elizabeth; her garden hat, gloves, and yellow silk stockings (the first pair worn in England); many of her letters and letters to her from Mary Queen of Scots.

There are articles belonging to other sovereigns here too: Charles I's cradle; Queen Anne's Chair of State; and a beautiful Posset Set which was a betrothal gift to Mary I and Philip of Spain.

HEALE HOUSE

A seventeenth century manor house at Woodford, four miles north of Salisbury, Wiltshire. Notable for having sheltered Charles II for about a week as he was trying to escape to France after the Battle of Worcester. He visited Stonehenge while he was here.

HEVER CASTLE

Kent. About 7 miles south of Sevenoaks. The childhood home of Anne Boleyn, and visited by Henry VIII as he was courting her. After the death of Anne's father Henry seized the castle and it became the home of Anne of Cleves, his fourth wife.

HOLDENBY HOUSE

Northamptonshire, nine miles north-west of Northampton. A property which once belonged to James I, and was used by both James I and Charles I. Charles was held here as guest-prisoner in 1647 but after his execution the house was demolished.

The present house was built in the nineteenth century, incorporating parts of the original building.

HOLYROOD HOUSE

Edinburgh. Royal Palace, still an official residence of British monarchs, founded by King David I in 1128, although after James VI left here to become King of England, no reigning monarch slept here until Queen Victoria came to the throne. Since then it has been visited by all British kings and queens and Queen Elizabeth II stays here for a fortnight each summer.

David Rizzio, secretary of Mary Queen of Scots, was murdered here in 1566. 'Bonnie Prince Charlie', the Young Pretender, lived and held his court here in 1745, making preparations to invade England and claim the throne.

HULL

Humbershire. The first act of defiance against Charles I in the Civil War occurred at Hull. The king tried to gain access to its arsenal but the town was a Parliamentarian stronghold and refused to let him in.

HURST CASTLE

Milford-on-Sea, Hampshire, about 18 miles east of Bournemouth. It was one of the last places of imprisonment of Charles I as he was taken from the Isle of Wight to Windsor.

KENILWORTH CASTLE

Warwickshire, about 4 miles north of Warwick. Many royal connections in the middle ages, but its main claim to fame was during Queen Elizabeth I's reign.

She gave the castle to Robert Dudley, Earl of Leicester, and he entertained her there in 1575 for three whole weeks, spending an astronomical sum on the lavish and spectacular 'Pleasures of Kenilworth'.

John Burbage was the organiser of these events and he made a fortune, shrewdly investing it in the construction of the first round theatre in London (in fact in the world). The Parliamentarian forces 'slighted' Kenilworth Castle in 1649 and it is now merely a picturesque ruin.

KENSINGTON PALACE

London, about $1^1/_2$ miles west of Hyde Park Corner. The original house was built about 1605 for the Earl of Nottingham. William III bought this 'Nottingham House', as it was called, as he suffered badly from asthma and found the air cleaner there than in Whitehall.

Christopher Wren and Nicholas Hawksmoor were called in to improve it, and William and Mary moved in at Christmas 1689. Both of these monarchs died here. Queen Anne built the Orangery, and she, too, died in the palace, as did George II.

Queen Victoria was born here in 1819, and Queen Mary, consort of George V was also born in the same room, in 1867.

Many minor royals have lived and still live in this palace, which is pleasantly informal, but which contains a great deal of royal memorabilia. Parts of the State Apartment are open to the public throughout the year.

KEW

Surrey, on the south bank of the Thames, about 6 miles from London. It was the future George II who bought a lodge here in 1719 and when he became king it was a comfortable country retreat for him, not too far from London.

His queen, Caroline, enjoyed adding a hermitage, dairy, temple and 'Merlin's Cave' much in the same way that Marie Antoinette added picturesque 'follies' to the gardes of Versailles. Frederick, Prince of Wales and his wife Augusta also lived here, and it was Princess Augusta who planned the Botanic Gardens, with its Orangery and Pagoda.

Her son, the future George III, spent much of his childhood here, and when he in turn became king he and his queen, Charlotte, lived here with their fifteen children in 'Kew Palace'.

The palace still survives as 'Kew's best kept secret' and has much of royal interest for visitors. Queen Charlotte's Cottage, a lovely thatched building, may also still be seen.

KINGSTON-UPON-THAMES

Surrey, about 10 miles south-west of London. In front of its modern Guildhall is the 'King's Stone' on which, or near which, seven Saxon Kings were crowned: Edward the Elder, Athelstan, Edmund I, Edred, Edwy, Edward the Martyr, and Ethelred II ('The Unready').

In this respect, the stone has something of the reputation of the 'Stone of Scone' which is to be found under the Coronation Throne in Westminster Abbey.

LEICESTER

About 100 miles north of London. An important city in the Midlands. Many kings and queens have come here over the centuries. Henry IV's first wife, Mary de Bohun, is buried in the church of St Mary in the Newarke. Henry IV himself often stayed in Leicester Castle, as did Henry V and Henry VI.

Richard III rode out from Leicester to his death at the Battle of Bosworth, and Henry VII (as he had just become) rode back into Leicester as victor.

Richard III's bones are somewhere here; perhaps, it has been supposed, now under one of the city's car parks.

Leicester was besieged by Royalist forces during the Civil War and King Charles's troops pillaged the city.

LINCOLN

Cathedral city about 142 miles north of London. William the Conqueror ordered its castle to be built, and his grandson, King Stephen, was captured here during the civil war with Matilda.

It was an important city, visited by many kings. Henry II gave himself a second coronation here; King John received homage from the Scottish King William I ('The Lion') here; Edward I held a parliament here; Edward II held another parliament here; and for various reasons most mediaeval kings were fêted or did business here. The cathedral is one of the finest in England.

LITTLE GIDDING

Cambridgeshire, about 12 miles south-west of Peterborough. The seventeenth century religious commune established by Nicholas Ferrar will be well known to readers of T.S.Eliot's *Four Quartets.*

A visitor can enter the tiny church of St John and remember that Charles I visited this community thee times: once in jubilation as he went to be crowned in Scotland in 1633; once as a regal visitor with his son Charles II in 1641; and finally in desperation at the end of the Civil War in November 1646, '...a broken king.'

This site is difficult to find, but has poignant associations.

LUDLOW CASTLE

Shropshire, about 32 miles north-west of Worcester. Its massive Norman castle was a famous stronghold near the Welsh border and many mediaeval kings had of necessity to stay here when in this part of the country. It was traditionally a residence of heirs to the throne – Princes of Wales.

It was from Ludlow that the young uncrowned King Edward V, aged 12, was escorted to London, to be murdered with his younger brother in the Tower of London.

Prince Arthur, elder brother of the future Henry VIII, lived here briefly with his wife Catherine of Aragon and died here aged only 15.

Henry VIII sent his nine-year-old daughter Mary to live here 1525-7; at the time she was heir to the throne, so it was a traditional place to send her. However, after this time Ludlow has had no close royal links.

LYME REGIS

Dorset, about 24 miles west of Dorchester. It was here that Charles II's illegitimate son the Duke of Monmouth landed, on 11 June 1685, to begin his campaign to oust his uncle, James II, from the throne.

His headquarters was at the Old George Inn, in Coombe Street (now burnt down). Several of his supporters were hanged here after the rebellion was quelled.

MALMESBURY

Wiltshire, 23 miles north of Bath. It was here that the Saxon King Athelstan lived and was buried in the abbey.

MARLBOROUGH HOUSE

London, near St James's Palace. It was built for and named after Sarah, Duchess of Marlborough. It has been used by many royal heirs and widows: the Prince Regent's daughter, Princess Charlotte; the widowed Queen Adelaide; Edward VII and Alexandra when they were Prince and Princess of Wales; and the widowed Queen Mary, consort of George V.

It is now used by visiting Commonwealth dignitaries.

NASEBY

A Northamptonshire village, about 7 miles south of Market Harborough. Scene of the decisive battle of the Civil War in which Oliver Cromwell defeated the royalist army led by Charles I, Prince Maurice and Prince Rupert.

Sadly, there is now a modern road running through this site, and there is nothing to see, but if you are in the vicinity it is worth going to see where a turning-point in British history took place.

NEWARK-ON-TRENT

Nottinghamshire, about 16 miles south-west of Lincoln. It was in this castle that King John died in 1216, having just lost all his treasures somewhere in the fens.

Rumour has it that he had been poisoned by a monk at Swineshead Abbey a few days earlier.

NEWBURY

Berkshire, about 20 miles south of Oxford. Apart from various visits by royalty to Donnington Castle (just north of the town), Newbury is historically famous for the two battles which took place there during the Civil War.

The First Battle of Newbury was fought in September 1643 just a little west of the town when the Parliamentarians forced Charles I and the Royalists to retreat to Oxford. However, Donnington Castle still held out against the Parliamentarians for over two years.

A Royalist army trying to relieve Donnington Castle clashed with Parliamentarians at the Second Battle of Newbury in April 1646. This second battle was somewhat indecisive, but the Cavaliers gave a good account of themselves.

NEWCASTLE-UPON-TYNE

The 'New Castle' was built by the Normans and in the early centuries of its existence it had great strategic importance in campaigns against the Scots and as royal headquarters during troubled times in the north.

Henry IV was here as he had to deal with the rebellious Archbishop Scrope, and Henry VII was here as he had to deal with the rebellious Lambert Simnel. Charles I was here as he had to deal with rebels everywhere.

Eventually the tables were turned and Charles himself was held here as hostage just before being escorted as a prisoner to Holdenby House (q.v.).

NEW FOREST

Hampshire, north of Southampton. Nearly a hundred thousand acres of woodland and heathland where deer, horses, cattle and pigs still roam freely.

There are many beauty spots and camping sites where holiday-makers can enjoy the forest which William the Conqueror enlarged and reserved for his personal hunting.

It is 'new' in that the Conqueror destroyed about twenty villages and evicted the Saxon peasants in order to create an uncluttered space for himself. Two of his sons were killed here: Richard, in a hunting accident in 1081, and William Rufus in a rather more sinister 'accident'.

The 'Rufus Stone' near Cadnam marks the spot where William II (Rufus) is supposed to have fallen.

NEWMARKET

Cambridgeshire, about 13 miles east of Cambridge. For centuries Newmarket has welcomed royalty to its horse-racing. James I introduced this sport into England and it was he who bought himself a house in the high street which gradually became enlarged and known as the 'Old Palace', used frequently by succeeding royalty right down to the time of 'Prinny' (the future George IV, who began the 'Prince's Stakes' here in the late eighteenth century), and Edward VII, who stayed in Palace House Mansion, which was what the former Old Palace had become in the late nineteenth century.

Nell Gwynne's House is in Palace Street – Charles II came here often, establishing royal stables and giving great impetus to this 'sport of kings'.

NORTHAMPTON

Northamptonshire, about 42 miles north-east of Oxford. It has seen many moments of royal high significance. Its Norman castle witnessed the clash between Henry II and Thomas Becket, after which Becket was exiled to France.

The captured William I of Scotland formally submitted to Henry II here in 1174. John quarrelled with the Pope's representative here. Simon de Montford briefly imprisoned Henry III here in 1265. Edward II and Edward III held parliaments here.

And Richard of Gloucester met his young nephew Edward V here, escorting him carefully to London so that he could murder him and become Richard III.

The royal history of Northampton is filled with incident, but there is little to see today. The castle has been destroyed. The most memorable relic of direct royal significance is the beautiful Eleanor Cross – probably the finest still remaining – just south of the town, at Hardingstone.

NORWICH

Norfolk, about 105 miles north-east of London. A beautiful cathedral city, visited on many occasions by royalty, especially on their way to the shrine at Walsingham.

Queen Elizabeth I made a memorable visit here in 1578 and was entertained with immense gusto. Perhaps the main importance in the distant past is that Boudicca, Queen of the Iceni, had her headquarters here.

NOTTINGHAM

County town of Nottinghamshire, 128 miles north of London. As with so many towns, William the Conqueror is responsible for building its castle. The early Norman and Plantagenet kings were frequently here.

Two episodes remain firmly embedded in many people's minds.The first was when Richard I gave Nottingham to his younger brother John, but excluded the castle itself from the gift. Then, when Richard was away on his crusade, the untrustworthy John seized the castle for his own. These were the days of Robin Hood and his merry men, living in nearby Sherwood Forest and striking terror into the heart of the Sheriff of Nottingham.

Of course, when Richard returned he quickly laid siege to the castle and brought John before a special council, accusing him of treason and forcing him to submit and apologise.

The second episode is less picturesque as we remember the sad, forlorn person of King Charles I struggling in the rain and wind to plant his royal standard on the mound outside the castle, as a kingly gesture to start the Civil War. There were few to cheer as the standard went up at 6.00 pm on 22nd August, 1642. Later, in 1647, Charles passed this way again, this time as prisoner.

But a third episode is also well worth remembering, for it was here that supporters of the 17-year-old King Edward III entered the castle through a secret passage in order to help him overthrow Queen Isabella (the 'She-Wolf of France'), and her lover Roger Mortimer. Mortimer was hanged; Isabella was put under house arrest for thirty-one years until her death in a Norman fortress at Castle Rising in Norfolk; and Edward seized the real reins of power at last.

Sadly, the Norman castle is no more, demolished in the Civil War, but a new seventeenth century building was put up on the site by William Cavendish, Duke of Newcastle. Visitors can see some fascinating items here, however, many dating back to mediaeval times.

NEWPORT

Isle of Wight. The old grammar school here was a lodging of Charles I and one of the schoolrooms was used by him during his negotiations with a group of commissioners as they drew up what was known as the Treaty of Newport.

In the church in the centre of the town is a pathetic and beautiful marble effigy of Charles's teenage daughter Elizabeth, also imprisoned in Carisbrooke Castle and who caught a fever and died there.

Surprisingly, it is a nineteenth-century monument. Queen Victoria had it made, more than 200 years after Elizabeth's death, as a token of respect for the poor child, caught up in those terrible events.

OSBORNE HOUSE

Isle of Wight. Anyone wishing to become fully acquainted with the life of Queen Victoria must visit Osborne House. Every square inch proclaims her presence: to visit Osborne is a fascinating experience.

When Queen Victoria first visited Old Osborne House with Albert she was completed captivated by the site. She wrote: "It is impossible to imagine a prettier spot – we have a charming beach quite to ourselves – we can walk anywhere without being followed or mobbed"

She and Albert bought the property in 1845. "I am delighted with the house," wrote the Queen in her diary. ". . . which is so complete and snug." Albert immediately set to work to re-design and rebuild it according to his own fastidious tastes. It was complete within a few years and here Victoria's growing family grew up.

The royal children were given a furnished 'Swiss Cottage' to play in and to learn housekeeping and cookery. It was perhaps the world's first 'Wendy House'.

Here Victoria spent the idyllic years of her married life, and when in 1861 Albert suddenly died, she spent the remaining 40 years of her widowhood here, expecting the whole world to come to her in her prolonged grief. And it was there that she died, cradled in the Kaiser's arms (her favourite grandchild) and surrounded by her family.

Accordingly, virtually nothing has changed. Shortly after his death she wrote: ". . . *his* wishes – *his* plans – about *everything*, his views about *every* thing are to be my *law!* And no human power will make me swerve from *what he* decided and wished."

Visitors should allow plenty of time to take everything in: it is crammed with Victoriana and apart from all the formal rooms we can also see her personal lift (worked by hand by a servant in the basement!), her shower and bathroom, the nursery suite, the Swiss Cottage and toy gardening-tools, and even Victoria's own private bathing-machine.

And among the pictures is the famous portrait of Victoria on horseback, attended by the notorious old rogue, John Brown.

Her successor, Edward VII, disliked the place and quickly gave it to the nation. For a while it was a Royal Naval College but this was closed. However, parts of it are still in use as a convalescent home.

OXFORD

University city, 56 miles north-west of London. Countless books have been written about Oxford and the great men and women who have have shared in its history. This book, however, must confine itself to royal connections.

It was fortified against the Danes by Edward the Elder in 911-121; Athelstan established a mint here in 925; and Canute held a Council of Saxons and Danes here.

The Empress Matilda made a spectacular escape from a tower of the Norman Castle during one winter's night as she was being besieged by King Stephen's armies in December, 1142. She was let down by ropes, wearing white clothes to camouflage herself in the winter landscape, crossed the frozen river by foot, and made her way to Wallingford, 13 miles away.

All this was well before anyone had ever heard of a university here. The scholars began to arrive in the 12th century and the first colleges were University College, founded by William of Durham in 1249; Balliol, founded by John de Balliol in 1262 as a penance for insulting William of Durham; and Merton, founded in 1260 by Walter de Merton.

These dates vary, and there is some dispute about which college actually *is* the oldest; some even claim that University College was founded by Alfred the Great! It is to be noted, however, that John de Balliol was the father of the Scottish king of that name. Henry I had a royal palace residence here, called Beaumont Palace, somewhere near where Beaumont Street exists today.

Henry II spent much time here and his sons Richard the Lionheart and King John were both born in this Beaumont Palace (which exists no longer). And in 1258, in Henry III's reign, a turning-point in English history occurred when 'The Provisions of Oxford' led to the formation of the beginnings of Parliament.

Queen's College was founded in 1340 by Robert of Eglesfield and named after Edward III's queen, Philippa of Hainault. She would have been about 26 at the time, but had already been queen for twelve years. The statue under the cupola over the entrance on the High Street, however, is that of Queen Caroline (wife of George II). She gave generously towards the improvement of the college in the eighteenth century.

As two queens have been involved in the establishment of this college it would perhaps be appropriate for the apostrophe to come after the 's', as in Queens' College Cambridge; but Oxford prefers just one.

Duke Humphrey, youngest brother of Henry V, gave his collection of books to the university, forming the basis of its library.

Oxford's importance during the Civil War was considerable, for it became Charles I's headquarters. He lived at Christ Church and his queen, Henrietta Maria, lived at Merton College.

Merton is also connected with royalty in that Charles II's mistress, Lady Castlemaine, gave birth to one of his illegitimate sons here.

Over the years, almost every monarch has visited Oxford for one purpose or another and two recent kings have received part of their education here.

Although Queen Victoria did not like Oxford, she and Albert sent their eldest son, the future Edward VII to Christ Church as an undergraduate in 1859. He lived in Frewen Hall, off Cornmarket Street, and stayed for four terms. In one of her letters, Victoria wrote: "Today dear Papa has gone to Oxford to see how Bertie is getting on in that old monkish place which I have a horror of."

Finally, the future Edward VIII spent two academic years, 1912-1914, in rooms in Magdalen's eighteenth century 'New Buildings'. The verdict of one don on the youthful prince was: "Bookish he will never be".

PERTH

Scotland, Tayside. Perth was the capital of Scotland until about 1452. Scone Palace is two miles to the north, a replacement of the original palace where, from 843 to 1296, Kings of Scotland were crowned on the Stone of Destiny, or Stone of Scone (See ***WESTMINSTER ABBEY***).

PETERBOROUGH

Cambridgeshire, about 85 miles north-east of London. Two queens were buried in the cathedral, but both tombs were torn up in the Civil War. Catherine of Aragon was buried in 1536, well away from London, where Henry VIII was then married to Anne Boleyn.

Mary Queen of Scots was buried here in 1587, after being beheaded at Fotheringhay, about 10 miles away. Mary's son, James I, had his mother's remains re-buried in Westminster Abbey.

PEVENSEY

East Sussex, 4 miles north-east of Eastbourne. The coastal site where William the Conqueror landed with his forces in 1066. A Norman castle was built here on the site of a previous Roman fort, and it has been the target of four sieges, involving William Rufus in 1088, King Stephen in 1147, Simon de Montfort in 1264-65, and Richard II's supporters in 1399.

The castle was manned against the Spanish Armada, and it was reinforced with extra defences in the Second World War. Clearly, it has strategic importance.

PLYMOUTH

Devon, about 42 miles south-west of Exeter. As with all major sea-ports, many royal visitors have passed through. Plymouth has seen the Black Prince; Catherine of Aragon; the Duke of Clarence (the future William IV); and Victoria and Albert.

PONTEFRACT CASTLE

West Yorkshire, about 11 miles south-east of Leeds. Inescapably linked with the death of Richard II, who was imprisoned here and who was probably murdered here on orders of Henry Bolingbroke after he had usurped the throne as Henry IV. Richard III created his son Prince of Wales here, and generally it was a useful royal castle because of its position as monarchs travelled north to Scotland.

The castle was severely damaged by Parliamentarian forces in the Civil War.

PORTSMOUTH

Hampshire, about 75 miles west of London. A great naval centre in the past, and a popular tourist centre for those who are interested in ships. Three ships are permanently on view: *HMS Victory, HMS Warrior* and more recently the fascinating remains of Henry VIII's famous war-ship, *Mary Rose*. Henry VIII himself saw this ship, the pride of his fleet, set off in calm water to engage a French fleet anchored off the Isle of Wight. To his horror, it keeled over and sank, with the loss of 700 men. In 1982 Prince Charles was present as it was raised from the ocean bed, and since that time it has been the object of intense care and investigation.

Portsmouth was the place where Charles I's favourite, the Duke of Buckingham, was stabbed. It was the landing-place of Charles II's wife-to-be, Catherine of Braganza. Any many monarchs subsequently visited the town as they made their various trips abroad.

Perhaps the most poignant sailing was made by Edward VIII, having just abdicated. He left Portsmouth on 12 December, 1936, newly created Duke of Windsor, into virtually permanent exile.

RICHMOND

North Yorkshire. About 13 miles south-west of Darlington. This was the *original* Richmond, where stands a Norman castle, and which gave rise to the title 'Earl of Richmond'.

The most famous Earl of Richmond was Henry, the victor at Bosworth, who became Henry VII, and it is this Henry who created his new palace at Sheen, re-naming it 'Richmond'. (See the next entry).

RICHMOND-UPON-THAMES

Surrey, about 8 miles west of London. Only the gatehouse now remains to be seen nowadays of the magnificent palace which stood here in former times, but it is worth recording that this was an important site where royalty once lived.

The old Sheen Palace was burnt down in 1497 and was completely rebuilt by Henry VII. When it was ready for occupation Henry renamed it 'Richmond' Palace. All the Richmond names around here owe their existence to this renamed palace, which one courtier called "an earthly and second Paradise, most glorious and joyful to consider and behold".

Henry VII died in his new palace; Henry VIII and Catherine of Aragon came here often; Mary I negotiated her marriage with Philip of Spain here; and Elizabeth loved the place, eventually dying here in 1603, possibly in a room just over the surviving gatehouse.

Richmond Park contains White Lodge, now the Royal Ballet School, where George V and Queen Mary lived when they were Duke and Duchess of York. It was in White Lodge that the future King Edward VIII was born; and it was here too that King George VI and Queen Elizabeth lived when they, in their turn, were Duke and Duchess of York.

ROCHESTER

Kent, about 30 miles south-east of London. The cathedral and the castle were both designed and built by William the Conqueror's bishop-architect, Gundulf. As a staging-post on the way to Canterbury it has seen many royal visitors, including Henry VIII, disguised, catching his first glimpse of Anne of Cleves, and being horrified at the sight.

ROMSEY

Hampshire, about 10 miles west of Winchester. A nunnery here was founded by King Edward the Elder about 907, and royal connections were strong for several hundreds of years. King Edgar refounded it in 966, and it became a place where royal daughters were brought up. Two daughters of Queen Margaret of Scotland were educated here, one of whom became Queen Matilda, wife of Henry I. The abbey was bought by the townsfolk for £100 at the time of the Dissolution of the Monasteries.

Nearby Broadlands House was the home of Earl Mountbatten of Burma, where two royal couples spent the first nights of their honeymoon: Queen Elizabeth II and the Duke of Edinburgh; and Prince Charles and Princess Diana.

RUFUS STONE

Hampshire, in the New Forest, about 10 miles west of Romsey. This stone marks the spot where, traditionally, King William II ('Rufus') was shot by an arrow. The stone is covered by a triangular iron monument which tells the story of the event. The king's body was taken by a local charcoal-burner to Westminster, and a plaque on a building in Bell Street, Romsey, reminds us of the probable route taken.

RUNNYMEDE

On the River Thames between Hampton Court and Windsor. It was, of course, the site of the signing of Magna Carta in 1215, when King John was forced to bow to the will of his barons. There is nothing to be seen dating from that time, but in 1957 the American Bar Association built a memorial to the occasion, and there is a memorial to President John Kennedy nearby, dedicated by Queen Elizabeth II in 1965.

The inscription reads: "This acre of English ground was given to the United States of America by the people of Britain in memory of John F. Kennedy".

ST ALBANS

Hertfordshire, about 27 miles north-west of London. Many royal visitors have come here, often as pilgrims coming to the shrine of St Alban, for the abbey church marks the site of his martyrdom.

Two battles took place here during the Wars of the Roses, the first of which, on 22 May, 1455, marked the opening of hostilities between the rebel Yorkists and the royal Lancastrian, Henry VI. In this engagement the Yorkists won and Henry VI was wounded and captured. The second battle, in 1461, was won by the Lancastrians, and for a while the tables were turned.

ST GEORGE'S CHAPEL, WINDSOR

Windsor, Berkshire. Built between 1475 and 1528, this is a superb example of late Gothic architecture. It was the inspiration of Edward IV, certainly his finest memorial, and he was the first of ten sovereigns to be buried here. Nowadays this is the usual burial-place of British monarchs.

Naturally, the memorials to these kings and their queens are of prime interest to tourists. One of the most memorable is the quaint money-box by the tomb of Henry VI, whose remains became an object of pilgrimage: pilgrims would put offerings in this box.

Also of particular interest are the effigies of Edward VII and Queen Alexandra, with the king's dog at his feet; and the effigies of George V and Queen Mary in startling white stone. And perhaps the most moving monument is that to Princess Charlotte, daughter of George IV, who died in childbirth.

But there is much more to see, and visitors must take their time to see everything, especially the magnificent choir and chancel.

The most recent burial was that of George VI, whose special Memorial Chapel was dedicated in 1969.

SALISBURY

Wiltshire, about 90 miles west of London. This is the city of 'New Sarum', built around the present cathedral, which was begun in 1220. An earlier city, 'Old Sarum', existed before that time on ancient circular earthworks about two miles to the north.

Old Sarum was a prehistoric earthwork fortified by Alfred the Great and of sufficient importance for William the Conqueror to choose it for a new diocese, shifting the see from Sherborne and building a new castle and cathedral here.

William the Conqueror summoned all his nobles here in 1086 and made them swear personal allegiance to him at the 'Oath of Salisbury'.

William Rufus and the early Norman kings frequently visited this hill-top city, but it was intolerably cramped for space and a new cathedral was built in meadows about two miles to the south, begun in 1220 and consecrated in 1258.

Henry III, probably the greatest patron of church architecture of all our monarchs, regularly visited the site to watch the progress of the building. He gave the timbers for the roof and tower, and attended the consecration of the new cathedral in 1258.

In the city of New Sarum (present-day Salisbury), Edward I held a parliament in 1297, as did Richard II in 1384. Richard III executed the rebel Duke of Buckingham in Salisbury market-place. Charles II and Catherine of Braganza spent a month here in 1665, escaping from the plague of London.

It was in Salisbury that James II's fortunes finally faded away, for when he arrived here in 1688 on his way to fight the invading William of Orange he suffered such constant nose-bleeds that he was forced to return to London; his commander-in-chief, John Churchill (future Duke of Marlborough) deserted him and went to support William (future William III) instead.

James I loved Salisbury, staying in a beautiful house in the Close opposite the west front of the Cathedral (the 'King's House') in which the city museum is now on view.

SANDRINGHAM

Norfolk, about 8 miles north-east of King's Lynn. This royal estate is much loved by the present family, who stay there regularly, especially at Christmas.

It is a relatively recent acquisition, having been purchased by the Prince of Wales (the future Edward VII) in 1862. As might be expected, it is filled with royal memorabilia, and is well worth visiting. Every member of the royal family since 1862 has lived or stayed here, often inviting foreign royalty as guests.

In the grounds is a cottage, 'York House', so named because it was given to the future George V while he was still the Duke of York. He and his wife, the future Queen Mary, lived there and it was here that the future George VI was born in 1895.

George V died here in 1936; George VI died here in 1952; and Princess Diana was born at Park House on the Sandringham estate in 1961.

SOUTHAMPTON

Hampshire, about 85 miles west of London. Over the centuries this seaport has inevitably witnessed the comings and goings of many kings. Situated where it is, their armies have set sail from here mostly to wage war against France.

Edward III set sail from Southampton on his way to fight at Crécy; and Henry V set sail from here on his way to Agincourt.

During the Second World War Southampton suffered terrible bomb damage, and George VI visited the town to see the devastation for himself. Royal memories are, sadly, very much in the distant past.

SOUTHWELL

Nottinghamshire, a cathedral city about 7 miles west of Newark. The cathedral is one of the glories of English architecture. The Saracen's Head Inn is where Charles I finally surrendered to the Scottish Covenanters on 5 May, 1646, thus ending the Civil War.

This same inn boasts that it has given accommodation to eight English kings: Richard I, John, Henry III, Edward III, Richard II, Edward IV, James I, and lastly Charles I.

STAMFORD

Lincolnshire, about 40 miles east of Nottingham. A beautiful stone-built town, filled with memories of the past. Edward II held a parliament here, and Richard II held a Great Council.

As it is on the main road to the north, it has been a major staging-post for everyone going to York and beyond; Henry VII; Henry VIII and Catherine Howard; Elizabeth I; James I; William III; Victoria and Albert.

One of the greatest Elizabethan houses, Burghley House, is just outside the town, and has attracted many royal visitors, including Princess Anne, the Princess Royal, who has enjoyed taking part in the horse trials in Burghley Park.

STAMFORD BRIDGE

North Yorkshire, a village 7 miles east of York. Site of the battle in 1066 in which King Harold fought the Norwegian invaders and killed their king, Harold Hardrada. Immediately afterwards he had to march south again to fight Duke William of Normandy at the Battle of Hastings.

SYON HOUSE

Brentford, Greater London. About 7 miles south-west of central London, and not far from Heathrow Airport. A stately house with many royal connections.

It was transformed in the 18th century and George III and George IV were both entertained here. But the main history of the pre-transformed house is linked with the Tudors.

Catherine Howard was kept virtual prisoner here after Henry had discovered her alleged infidelities; and it was from here that she went to her death.

The body of Henry VIII was brought here overnight on the way to Windsor. Protector Somerset lived here, guardian of Edward VI. And it was here at Syon House that Lady Jane Grey was proclaimed Queen of England. She set out from here, expecting to go to her coronation, but ended in the Tower of London instead.

It was Henry V who had originally founded Syon Abbey, one of two religious houses (the other was at Sheen), to expiate his father's connivance in the murder of Richard II.

Like many abbeys it fell into private hands at the time of the Dissolution of the Monasteries.

TEWKESBURY

Gloucester, about 11 miles north of Gloucester. Scene in 1471 of the last battle in the Wars of the Roses, in which the Yorkists were victorious and the Lancastrian Edward Prince of Wales, son of Henry VI, was killed. He is buried in Tewkesbury Abbey, a huge building begun in Norman times.

TOWTON

North Yorkshire. 12 miles south-west of York. In 1461, ten years before the Battle of Tewkesbury, the Lancastrian army was defeated by the Yorkists in one of the bloodiest engagements ever to take place in England, fought in a snowstorm.

TUNBRIDGE WELLS

Kent. A spa town 18 miles south-west of Maidstone. When it was fashionable to take spa water Tunbridge Wells enjoyed much royal patronage. Charles I and Henrietta Maria came to enjoy the waters; so did Charles II; and so did Anne, the future queen, who brought her ailing little boy the Duke of Gloucester, hoping the waters would strengthen him; George II and Victoria also came here, and Edward VII gave permission for the town to use the title 'Royal' Tunbridge Wells.

The main church in Royal Tunbridge Wells, opened in 1678 has the unusual dedication: it is known as the Church of King Charles-the-Martyr. This shows how strong the Royalist feeling was after the Restoration of the monarchy.

TUTBURY CASTLE

Staffordshire, 11 miles south-west of Derby. Now in ruins, this Norman castle was home and prison of Mary Queen of Scots on two occasions (1569 and 1585) but she found conditions here too bad for her health and had to be moved to Chartley Hall.

WALSINGHAM

Norfolk, 5 miles north of Fakenham. The famous shrine here was a place of pilgrimage for hundreds of thousands, including virtually every king from the time of its foundation in the eleventh century to the time of its destruction in 1538-9.

Even Henry VIII, before he began his dissolution of the monasteries, once walked barefoot for over a mile to visit the holy shrine. A new shrine, completed in 1937, is now to be found there.

TOWER OF LONDON

London, Tower Hill. If a visitor to England has time for only one place of royal associations, then perhaps the Tower of London is the top priority. It is in fact a complex of twenty towers, nineteen of which are built in a huge circle around the main fortress in the middle, which is called the White Tower, because at one time it was coated with whitewash.

The White Tower stands on the site of William the Conqueror's first wooden fort, constructed quickly immediately after he had settled here, and built around ruins of an earlier Roman fortification. In 1078 William ordered the building of the present massive stone fortress, which stands 90ft. high and has walls 15ft. thick at the base. No one has ever captured the Tower of London!

This main fortress has been added to over the centuries: tower after tower, with inner walls, outer walls, a moat, a chapel, a palace, and so on. It is a complex series of buildings, and it is best to study a plan before you arrive.

The whole collection of towers is permeated with royal associations. The main White Tower served as the royal residence for all mediaeval kings, but of course became less used as other palaces were built.

On Tower Green Anne Boleyn, Catherine Howard and Lady Jane Grey were beheaded, and they are buried in the nearby chapel of St Peter ad Vincula.

Other towers with special royal memories are the Wakefield Tower, in which Henry VI was murdered; the Bloody Tower, in which the young princes, sons of Edward IV, were most probably murdered on orders of Richard III; and the Beauchamp Tower was the prison of Lord Guilford Dudley, who perhaps scratched the name of 'Jane' twice on the wall here.

'Traitors' Gate' was the entrance through which prisoners were brought in from boats on the Thames. It was through this waterside gate that the future Queen Elizabeth I was forced to come, weeping and protesting, as her half-sister Queen Mary I ordered her detainment in the Tower.

In its time the Tower has acted as fortress, palace, storehouse, arsenal, treasure, mint, prison, and even zoo. Henry III kept leopards, a polar bear, an elephant and lions there. In fact animals were here until 1834, when they were sent to help set up the new zoo in Regent's Park.

WESTMINSTER ABBEY

London. In Westminster Abbey you are physically nearer to more kings and queens than anywhere else. Three kings are particularly associated with its construction: Edward the Confessor, who began it and who is buried behind the altar; Henry III, who greatly enlarged it in the 13th century and gave a new shrine to house the Confessor's bones; and Henry VII, who began the Lady Chapel with its magnificent fan-vaulting in the early 16th century.

Apart from Edward V (murdered) and Edward VIII (abdicated) every English King and Queen has been crowned in Westminster Abbey since its very beginning: in 1066 Edward the Confessor was buried here shortly after its consecration and within a few days his successor Harold II became the first king to be crowned here.

Later the same year, on Christmas Day, William the Conqueror sealed his victory by being crowned in the same church as his Saxon predecessor.

Next to the Confessor's shrine is the Coronation Chair, ordered to be made by Edward I to enclose the precious Stone of Scone which he had captured in his Scottish campaign.

His son, Edward II, was the first to be crowned in this Coronation Chair, on 25 February, 1308, and since then it has been used at every coronation.

There are so many royal tombs. It is hardly necessary to list them all. Gradually, St George's Chapel, Windsor, became the main burial place for our monarchs, and George II was the last king to be buried here, in 1760.

Apart from funerals and coronations, Westminster Abbey has witnessed many other scenes and events. The Chapter House was used for meetings of the king's council and for early parliaments; Henry IV died in the Jerusalem Chamber; Queen Elizabeth Woodville, wife of Edward IV, sought sanctuary here and actually gave birth here (her baby was 'Edward of the Sanctuary' – the future Edward V who was murdered in the Tower); and royal weddings have taken place here, including those of the future George VI and Elizabeth Bowes-Lyon, and of the future Elizabeth II and the Duke of Edinburgh.

WESTMINSTER PALACE

London. It is still common to talk of the 'Palace of Westminster' when referring to the Houses of Parliament. It is something of a misnomer, because the actual palace, which had stood here since the time of William the Conqueror, was destroyed in the fire of 1834. In its time it had been the principal palace of every king from Norman times until the Tudors.

William Rufus had great ambitions to build a vast palace here, and Westminster Hall, which survives today, is a part of that scheme.

Westminster Hall has been central to the history of the country, scene of celebrations and drama. It is 73 metres long and 20 metres wide. Many kings have lain in state here, including George V and George VI; it was the setting for coronation banquets until 1821; the usurping Henry IV was acclaimed king here; Charles I was put on trial and condemned by the revolutionary court in 1649.

Oliver Cromwell, naturally enough, was never crowned, but it was here in Westminster Hall that he was formally created 'Lord Protector'. And at the time of the restoration his body was dug up, decapitated, and his head was hung up and put on public view here for twenty years.

The new Palace of Westminster, designed by Charles Barry, was opened by Queen Victoria in 1852.

WHITEHALL PALACE

London. Although there are many important buildings here, the old Whitehall has gone for ever. It was an enormous, sprawling area, filled with all sorts of buildings.

Henry VIII acquired the site and its 'York Place' from Cardinal Wolsey, and the Tudors and Stuarts lived here in great state.

William III preferred Kensington, and Whitehall itself was virtually totally destroyed by fire in 1698.

Only the Banqueting House remains, and even that is a part of the new palace built for James I.

(See ***BANQUETING HOUSE***).

WINCHESTER

Hampshire. About 72 miles west of London. Winchester was the ancient Saxon capital of England. Many Saxon kings lived, ruled, died, and were buried in Winchester's earlier cathedral, known as 'Oldminster'. When the Normans came and built the present cathedral they pulled down its Saxon predecessor, and transferred the bones of the Saxon kings. Here they still lie in mortuary chests clearly on view near the altar.

Edward the Confessor was crowned here in 1043, the last coronation to take place in any place other than Westminster Abbey. William II (Rufus) was buried here; and his brother Henry I seized the treasury here, making sure of his claim to the throne.

Much damage was wrought to the Saxon city during the civil war between Stephen and Matilda. Bishop Henry, brother of King Stephen, succeeded in destroying virtually all the Saxon city in his zeal to defeat Matilda. Henry III ('Henry of Winchester') was born and christened in the cathedral font; he built the Great Hall still on view at the top of the High Street.

Henry IV married Joan of Navarre in the cathedral in 1403; Henry V passed through here on his way to Agincourt; Henry VII was anxious that his Queen should give birth here, which she duly did in 1486. The baby was christened Arthur in the cathedral.

Queen Mary I and Philip of Spain were married here; James held court at Wolvesey Palace; and Charles I was formally received here as he was escorted on his way from Hurst Castle to trial in London.

The last monarch to be closely associated with the city was Charles II, who ordered Wren to design a new palace for him here. It was almost completed when Charles died in 1685, but his successors were not interested in it and it became a barracks, burnt down in 1894.

In 1979 Queen Elizabeth II distributed the Royal Maundy at a service which celebrated the 900th anniversary of the consecration of the Norman cathedral.

There is so much to see in Winchester that visitors need to return again and again to take in all its beauty and interest. Royal objects to see here include: the great statue of Alfred the Great, dominating the High Street; the cathedral, which contains the famous mortuary chests of the Saxon kings, statues of James I and Charles I, the chair used by Mary I at her wedding here; and the huge design for a Versailles-type palace and gardens prepared for Charles II, which hangs in the city museum.

The remains of Wolvesey Palace, are worth visiting, although they are in ruins (destroyed by Oliver Cromwell). This was the palace of the bishops of Winchester, but was also used frequently by royal visitors, including Philip of Spain, as he dressed himself before his wedding in the cathedral.

WINDSOR CASTLE

Windsor, Berkshire. William the Conqueror founded it, and it has grown over the centuries. It was Henry II who first began the very distinctive Round Tower. Here the future Edward III was born, and later when he became king he founded the Order of the Garter here in 1344. Henry V conceived the notion that to be born here would prove unlucky for his son, the future Henry VI. Perhaps he was right!

Royal associations with Windsor Castle are so numerous that it would be impossible to list. George III, in his madness, died here. So did William IV and Prince Albert. But on the whole the castle has remained very much a place of royal residence, away from London, and yet near enough to be convenient to return there quickly.

Much of the splendour of the interior was the inspiration of George IV, who personally supervised an extensive rebuilding programme in the 1820's. It was then that the Round Tower was raised.

In 1992, the "Annus horribilis" of Queen Elizabeth II, a serious fire damaged some of the interior.

YORK

North Yorkshire, about 208 miles north of London. One of the greatest cities in England. Roman emperors lived and ruled here, and it was in Eboracum (their name for York) that Constantine the Great was proclaimed Emperor in 306 AD.

It was the capital of the Kingdom of Northumbria, and its King Edwin was converted to Christianity here in 627, beginning York's long association with the church. Struggles with Danes and Norsemen filled the pre-conquest centuries, leading William the Conqueror to build two castles here to help his Norman barons keep order.

Virtually every mediaeval king was forced to come here on various matters of business, and Edward III in particular found it convenient to regard it as his administrative centre, living here and making it his home. In fact, he married his wife, Philippa of Hainault in the Minster, and one of his sons, William of Hatfield, is buried there.

York had no love for the Lancastrian Henry IV, particularly after he had executed its Archbishop Scrope. And in the Wars of the Roses naturally it was a Yorkist centre receiving Edward IV in raptures after his success at the bloody Battle of Towton. Edward's brother, Richard III, was also immensely popular here.

ROYAL CEREMONIES

Tourists and visitors to Britain are often intrigued by the colourful royal customs and traditions surrounding the monarch. Here are some of the events which attract much popular interest.

CHANGING THE GUARD

Outside Buckingham Palace — *Daily at 11.30 (including Sundays)*

This is one of the sights of London. The troops taking part are chosen from one of the five regiments of Foot Guards: the Grenadier Guards, the Coldstream Guards, the Scots Guards, the Irish Guards, or the Welsh Guards.

The men of the duty guard march from Wellington Barracks or Chelsea Barracks to Buckingham Palace accompanied by a band, which plays in the palace forecourt during the ceremony of Changing the Guard.

The Grenadier Guards gained their name from the fact that they defeated Napoleon's Grenadier Guards at the Battle of Waterloo. The Coldstream Guards are named after their march from Coldstream, near Berwick-on-Tweed, to mount an extraordinary guard for Charles II in 1660 at the time of the restoration. The Scots Fusilier Guards became known as the Scots Guards in 1661. Queen Victoria commanded the formation of the Irish Guards in 1900. The Welsh Guards were formed in 1915. All these form the 'Brigade of Guards', who serve as personal bodyguards of the reigning monarch.

If you want to identify which regiment is on guard, notice the buttons on their tunics. The Grenadiers have single buttons; the Coldstream Guards have buttons in pairs; the Scots, buttons in threes; the Irish in fours; and the Welsh in fives.

If the Royal Standard is flying from Buckingham Palace signifying that the Sovereign is in residence, then there will be a guard of four sentries; but if the Sovereign is away from London there will be a guard of only two.

There are usually many sight-seers at this ceremony – a free spectacle – so it is advisable to arrive early to secure a good vantage-point.

The Quadrangle, Windsor Castle — ***Daily at 10.00 whenever the Queen is in residence at Windsor Castle***

Another ceremony of Changing the Guards takes place at Windsor whenever the Queen is in residence, also open to public view, and free.

MOUNTING THE GUARD

Horse Guards, Whitehall, London — *Every weekday at 11.00 am (Sundays at 10.00 am)*

This ceremony is another popular sight, enjoyed by visitors to London. The guard is provided by the Household Cavalry: either the Royal Horse Guards or the Life Guards.

You can recognise which is which by their uniform: the Life Guards wear scarlet uniforms, white metal helmets with white horsehair plumes, and sit on white sheepskin saddles. The Royal Horse Guards wear deep-blue tunics, white metal helmets with red horsehair plumes, and their sheepskin saddles are black.

The ceremony reminds us that Horse Guards Arch was originally the entrance to St. James's Palace, and is the oldest of royal doorways. Only royalty may come through this, and the Queen drives through it when she is going to Westminster for the State Opening of Parliament.

There is another, less spectacular 'guard mounting' at St. James's Palace, the Tower of London, and Windsor Castle. The Mounting of the Guards at Whitehall, however, is the only ceremony where the cavalry perform the duty.

TROOPING THE COLOUR

Horse Guards Parade — *Annually, each June*

This annual ceremony marks the Queen's official birthday. Strictly speaking the title of this event should be the Queen's Birthday Parade, but everyone knows it as 'Trooping the Colour' and crowds turn out every year to watch it.

It was Queen Victoria who began the idea of an 'official birthday' and the custom has been retained ever since, mainly because the summer is a better time of year to hold this elaborate military display of marching and counter-marching. The term 'trooping' means 'saluting by beat of drum', and the 'colour' is another name for the flag or standard. The origin of 'trooping' a 'colour' was simply the practical one of reminding soldiers what flag they were supposed to follow – a practical visual sign of the rallying-point in battle.

Usually, about 2,000 men and 200 horses take part in this annual ceremony.

ROYAL VISITS TO THE CITY OF LONDON

The City of London is quite distinct from the City of Westminster, and whenever the Sovereign crosses the boundary into the City of London he or she is met by the Lord Mayor of London, usually at the site of the former Temple Bar, now marked by a Griffin.

The ceremony which now takes place involves the Lord Mayor's presenting the City's Pearl Sword to the Sovereign, who symbolically touches it in acceptance, and then returns it to the Lord Mayor. The City thus publicly demonstrates its allegiance.

THE STATE OPENING OF PARLIAMENT

Procession from Buckingham Palace to Westminster

Every Year in November or after a General Election

Symbolically, this is the perfect example of the way in which our British constitutional monarchy works. The State Opening of Parliament takes place in the House of Lords, not because this is the grander of the two Houses of Parliament, but because the sovereign has no physical connection whatsoever with the House of Commons. No monarch has been allowed to enter the House of Commons since Charles I made his unfortunate attempt to enter it and arrest MPs who had displeased him, an act which led finally to the Civil War in the seventeenth century.

The annual State Opening of Parliament involves a procession from Buckingham Palace to Westminster, and this also embodies a powerful visual message, for the Sovereign is preceded by a coach bearing the Imperial State Crown and other symbols of authority. The coach is lit from within so that all can see: so the message is clear – the office of the crown is more important than the person who wears it. The monarch follows behind in another coach, taking second place.

Once the Queen has arrived at Westminster the Imperial State Crown is placed on her head in an antechamber to the House of Lords, known as the Robing Room, and she then ceremonially enters the Chamber, where she will deliver the 'Queen's Speech'. This again is symbolic, for everyone knows that she herself does not write it. It contains the proposed legislation which the Government intends to introduce in the forthcoming year. Clearly the Government is 'in charge' of this proposed legislation, having itself written the Queen's Speech; nevertheless these proposals are openly and publicly declared before everyone, including the Lords and Members of 'Her Majesty's Opposition', who will have the power to debate and perhaps amend the proposed legislation; and the proposals are spoken by the Sovereign, who physically represents the authority by which all this is done.

Members of the House of Commons attend this ceremony in the House of Lords, being summoned from their own Chamber by an official known as 'Black Rod'. Once again, symbolism is enacted, for as he approaches the door of the Commons, that door is ritually slammed in his face and he has to knock three times to 'persuade' the MPs to open it up. The symbolism emphasises the fact that even the Queen's messenger has no 'right' of entry.

Power is with the people, not with kings or queens.

The public is admitted, but space is very limited. The procession through the streets, of course, is a splendid spectacle, and the entire proceedings are nowadays always shown on television.

THE ROYAL MAUNDY

Alternate years, either in Westminster Abbey or in another cathedral outside London

Each Maundy Thursday

Every year on Maundy Thursday (the day before Good Friday) the Sovereign ceremonially distributes coins to 'the well-deserving poor'. Special silver pennies are minted for this ceremony and the Queen gives as many coins as she has years, plus one for 'the Year of Grace', to each recipient. Those who receive this gift must be over sixty-five, and are chosen from all Christian denominations by the clergy of the diocese in which that year's Maundy Ceremony is taking place. They are chosen because of their years of Christian service.

The ceremony goes back to mediaeval times, when monarchs used to wash the feet of the poor and give them gifts of food and clothing. (The word 'maundy' comes from the Latin *'mandatum'*, 'commandment' – 'A new commandment I give unto you, that you love one another' – John 13:34). James II was the last monarch actually to wash feet of the poor, but William III fastidiously delegated the task to his almoner and later monarchs abandoned the practice altogether.

This ceremony was the first public engagement undertaken by Queen Elizabeth II as Queen, just two months after the death of her father George VI in 1952, and she began the practice of taking the custom to cathedrals outside London.

OTHER ROYAL OCCASIONS

Remembrance Sunday

The Remembrance Day ceremony and parade is held at the Cenotaph in Whitehall. The Queen leads the nation in remembering the dead in the two World Wars on a Sunday near to the original Armistice Day, 11 November, at 11.00 am.

The Garter Ceremony

Takes place in June every year in St. George's Chapel, Windsor. The public are allowed to see the colourful procession from the Castle to St. George's.

The Royal Tournament

A military tournament held at Earl's Court in July.

The Braemar Gathering

Highland games, including Scottish dancing and Highland contests such as 'Tossing the Caber', held at Braemar, Aberdeenshire, each September.

Royal Salutes

There are two main firing stations: Hyde Park and the Tower of London. Royal Salutes (41 guns) are fired on the Queen's official birthday in June, her true birthday (21 April), and the anniversaries of her Accession (6 February) and Coronation (2 June). Other royal and state occasions are also marked by gun salutes.

TELEPHONE NUMBERS OF PLACES OF INTEREST

Many historic houses and castles are open only from April to October, but there are some which are open all the year round. As opening times are always subject to change, here are contact phone numbers, correct at time of publication.

Intending visitors to these places of interest are advised to check in advance, to avoid disappointment.

Alnwick Castle
01665 510777

Arundel Castle
01903 883136/882173

Audley End House
01799 522399

Balmoral
0171 607 1098

Bamburgh Castle
01668 214208

Banqueting House
0171 839 8918

Bath Tourist Information Centre
01225 462831

Beaulieu Abbey
01590 612345

Berkeley Castle
01453 810332

Boscobel House
01902 850244

Bosworth Field Visitor Centre
01455 290429

Brighton Pavilion
01273 603005

Buckingham Palace
0171 9304832

Cambridge Tourist Information Centre
01223 322640

Canterbury Tourist Information Centre
01227 766567

Carisbrooke Castle
01983 522107

Carlisle Castle
01228 591922

Chatsworth House
01246 582204

Chester Tourist Information Centre
01244 324324 extn. 2111

Colchester Castle
01206 712481

Corfe Castle
01929 481294

Coventry Tourist Information Centre
01203 832311

Dover Castle
01304 201628

Durham Tourist Information Centre
0191 384 3720

Exeter Tourist Information Centre
01392 265297

Glastonbury Abbey
01458 832267

Gloucester Tourist Information Centre
01452 421188

Greenwich
0181 858 4422
Hampton Court Palace
0181 977 8441
Hatfield House
01707 262823
Kensington Palace
0171 937 9561
Kew Palace
0181 940 3321
Leicester
Tourist Information Centre
01533 511300/532353
Lincoln
Tourist Information Centre
01522 529828/512971
Ludlow Castle
01584 873947
Newbury District Museum
01635 30511
Newcastle-upon-Tyne
Tourist Information Centre
0191 261 0691
New Forest Visitors' Centre, Lyndhurst
01703 282269
Newmarket Tourist Information Centre
01638 719000
Northampton
Tourist Information Centre
01604 22677
Norwich
Tourist Information Centre
01603 666071
Nottingham
Tourist Information Centre
01602 470661
Osborne House
01983 200022
Oxford
Tourist Information Centre
01865 726871
Peterborough Cathedral
01733 555098
Portsmouth
Tourist Information Centre
01705 826722
Rochester
Tourist Information Centre
01634 843666
Romsey (Broadlands)
01794 516878
St Albans
Tourist Information Centre
01727 864511
St Paul's Cathedral, London
0171 248 2705
Salisbury
Tourist Information Centre
01722 334956
Sandringham House
01553 772765
St. George's Chapel Windsor
01753 865538
Stamford
Tourist Information Centre
01780 55611
Syon House
0181 560 0881
Tewkesbury
Tourist Information Centre
01684 295027
Tower of London
0171 709 0765
Westminster Abbey
0171 222 5152
Winchester
Tourist Information Centre
01962 848180/840500
Windsor
Tourist Information Centre
01753 852010
York
Tourist Information Centre
01904 621756

INDEX OF KINGS AND QUEENS

. . . AND FINALLY

. . . If you should ever be called upon to meet the Queen and talk to her, the correct form of address is 'Ma'am' – to rhyme with 'ham', not 'harm'.

The term 'Majesty' was not used before the reign of Henry VIII. Before that time Henry IV was referred to as 'His Grace'; Edward IV was known as 'High and Mighty Prince'; Henry VII was 'His Grace' or 'His Highness'. 'His Sacred Majesty' was used for some later kings, but nowadays this has been changed to 'His Most Excellent Majesty', or in the case of our present Queen, 'Her Most Excellent Majesty'.

The full title of Queen Elizabeth II is, however:

Elizabeth the Second, by the Grace of God of the United Kingdom of Great Britain and Northern Ireland and her other Realms and Territories, Queen, Head of the Commonwealth, Defender of the Faith.

VIVAT REGINA